Jack Rose's Lowestoft Life

First published 1991 by Panda Books
117 High Street, Lowestoft, Suffolk.

Printed in England by Richardson Printing Ltd
Units 31-33 Colville Road Works, Oulton Broad, Suffolk

Typeset by P.S. Typesetting
Unit 6 Colville Road Works, Oulton Broad, Suffolk

ISBN 0 9507775 9 5

Jack Rose's Lowestoft Life

Panda Books
PUBLISHING

This book is dedicated to
Mrs Ruth Scollard
Head Teacher
Roman Hill County Primary School

I shall pass through this world but once, therefore any good that I may do, or any Kindness I may show, let me do it now, let me not neglect it, for I shall not pass this way again.

Carlyle

Preface

I have been asked a number of times about writing my autobiography, but being an ordinary working man I wasn't sure how to go about it. However, when my friend Ivan Bunn agreed to help we came up with so much material that we hadn't room to use it all. I hope you will enjoy this book and perhaps more can be written at another time.

I would especially like to thank Ivan Bunn for all the work he put into helping me produce the manuscript and my friends at Panda Books for their encouragement and work in preparing the book for publication.

Over the years people have given or lent me photographs and I am forever in their debt. On this occasion I would particularly wish to acknowledge Mr D Bird, Mr K Day and Mrs S Hoad who have loaned photographs for inclusion in this book.

Finally, I must thank the people of Lowestoft whose interest in my work is an ever-present source of encouragement.

Jack Rose,
Lowestoft,
October 1991.

My Family

Our family had been fishermen for generations and were known as the 'Mike' Roses. My grandfather Henry, always called George, originally came from the Beach although he lived in Factory Street for a time. He was one of four children and when his mother (my great-grandmother) died, his father married a widow with four children of her own and proceeded to have seven more. All the boys slept in the front bedroom and the girls slept in the back, the old couple sleeping downstairs. When another baby came along they made the old copper into a cradle – just packed it out with pillows and that's where the baby slept!

My maternal grandfather, Robert George Draper, was skipper of a smack and was drowned in Lowestoft harbour, leaving my grandmother, Susannah Cossey Draper, *née* Redgrave, a young widow. No one seems to know quite how grandfather met his death. It was surmised that attempting to jump from his boat onto the quayside, he missed his footing and fell between the boat and the quay wall, banging his head as he went down. All they found on the quayside was his hat and kit-bag. Grandmother Draper was left to bring up her four children, Bob, George, Gertrude and Beatrice alone. Fate was unkind to this poor woman for many years later in 1941 she and her sister were killed in St Leonard's Road during a German bombing raid on the town.

Delving further into my family history, both sides appear to have had connections with the old China Factory that stood in Crown Street where Windsor and Newton's factory stands today. My father, Charles Edward, is said to be descended from old Thomas Rose who was a china painter. My grandmother also had connections with the factory through the Regrave family who were employed there during the eighteenth century. In fact there is a Lowestoft china birth plate still in existence made for a Susannah Redgrave.

It was on 24th January 1926 that I came into the world, born at 17 Clapham Road, Lowestoft the second son of Charles Edward and Beatrice Victoria Redgrave Rose, *née* Draper, and christened Jack Edmund. I was born into a dedicated lifeboat and fishing family who, like many more families during that era, were poor and faced much hardship.

At the time that I came into this world Mother and Father were in what in those days were known as 'rooms' – people let out part of their house to others in order to supplement their income. The 'rooms' in which I was born were rented by my father's aunt, Hetty Turrell (sister to my Granny Rose) and her fisherman husband Ollie. Also living there were my cousins Stella, Richard and Ollie Turrell. So, what with this family of five, me, my parents and my two brothers, George and Kenny, there were ten of us crammed into the one small terraced house.

My great grandfather — James 'Mike' Rose, yawlman, beachman, fisherman and lifeboatman

Grandad Rose with my brother George (back), my sister Meryl and brother Charlie (front right). I was at Lound delivering newspapers when this photograph was taken.

My father (centre front) with his brothers. Back row from left: John, Arco, Bert. Front row: George, Charles, Harry. Another brother, William, had been killed, aged only twelve, by a horse and cart in Gun Lane.

My mother, Beatrice

My father, Charles, longshoreman, fisherman, lifeboatman.

My brother George and I playing pirates in front of 17 Clapham Road (1931).

I well remember old Nanna Turrell, as we lovingly called her. She was a grand old lady and I called her 'Nanna' up to the day she died. She was tough, as all old ladies of her generation had to be, but she had a heart of gold and would soon come to our assistance should we need it. I remember once, when my brother Georgie and I were watching the men working in 'Watling's Yard' in Clapham Road, a bloke came and chased us away because of the horses going in and out of the yard. I must have said something to him because he grabbed me and put me into one of the barrels standing nearby. My brother ran to Nanna's – only three or four houses away – and told her what had happened. She was baking at the time and grabbing her rolling-pin she came hurrying after the villain who had put one of her precious grand-children into a barrel and gave him a right telling off, threatening him with the rolling-pin.

I remember being taken by Nanna to the Royal Plain where horse brakes, landaus and pony and traps were all lined up ready to take visitors and locals alike for a ride. Then there were charabanc trips and the horses and carriages of Watling's Stables at the rear of the *Clapham Hotel.* These were known as 'jingles' owing to the small bells which hung around the horses and parts of the harness.

Granny Rose's maiden name was Spillings. She was born at Benacre and some of her relations still lived there. In particular I remember her sister Liza who lived in Benacre Street with great-grandfather Spillings. Occasionally for a treat we would be taken to visit great-grandfather who was a very old gentleman with a long white beard which almost reached the floor when he was seated. When we entered their cottage at Benacre I was plonked onto a chair and told to speak when spoken to or otherwise hold my tongue.

Meals there were served in dead silence with grace being said first, after which all that could be heard was the rattling of knives and forks and the munching of food. When the grown-ups had finished eating we were allowed to get down from the table and go out into the garden where there was an old well. We used to love to drop stones down the well and listen to the splash as they hit the water. We knew that we were not supposed to do this and every time we dropped a stone into the well we waited for the voice which we knew, sooner or later, would roar out telling us to stop. As soon as this happened we would troop indoors to apologise for what we had done.

Sadly my little brother Kenny died in 1930 and soon after Kenny's death my grandfather lost his wife Agnes.

Not long after her death we moved to a large old house at No 2 Old Nelson Street, where subsequently my brother Charlie and sister Meryl were born. Grandfather Rose had got enough money together to get a mortgage on this house by giving up fishing for about three years and working away on a telegraph ship, laying cables. This house has long since gone and the new police station stands on the site. The house itself was a three-storey Victorian property with a front door below ground-level so that anyone calling had to descend a flight of steps. In the front room, which was used as a bed-sitter, lived my father's brother, John Rose, with his wife Nellie (*née* Ecclestone of Somerleyton) and their son Roy.

My family, together with grandfather, occupied the 'middle room' as it was called then. From there you had to descend another flight of steps to reach the basement which consisted of a kitchen, wash-house and scullery. In the kitchen area was a massive old cooking stove above which were enormous great ratchet hooks which could be pulled outwards and upon which whole carcases of meat could be hung. At the bottom of the yard, there were three sheds in which Granfer kept all the fishing gear and outside the front of the house was a great big board which said 'Henry G. Rose, 2nd Cox'n, lifeboat.'

My Granfer was only small but as hard as nails. Despite this he had a heart of gold. It was he who bought my first pair of long trousers, grey flannel serge, on the Plain for three shillings and sixpence a pair.

Although we all loved old Granfer dearly he didn't escape our pranks. I particularly remember one November 5th during the 1930s when we were sitting after tea with our scrapbooks and we thought we heard the lifeboat maroon go off. Up jumped grandfather, who was one of the lifeboat crew, and away he went like a greyhound running all the way down to the North Pier where the lifeboat used to be moored, only to find that it was a false alarm! Home he came again, puffing and panting, and flopped down in his favourite wooden rocking-chair. He then undid his boot laces and settled down again. By this time my brother and I were working on a 'piece' rug made from strips torn from old clothing, pulled with a special needle through sacking which was then sewn up with string.

When Granfer had settled-down and dozed off, twiddling his thumbs as usual, I got the string and with the help of my brother passed the string through the eyes of his boots and tied the ends round the chair legs. About half-an-hour later the maroons did go off and so did Granfer as he jumped up and fell flat on his face! He got up, said a few choice words, and with Mother's help pulled his feet out of his boots and away he went in his stockinged feet. After he had gone Mother told me off and boxed my ears and sent me to bed. In the morning I had to go to Granfer and say that I was sorry but it was two or three days before we were on speaking terms again.

Towards the latter days of Granfer's life his eyes started to go and my brother or I used to have to walk him to Lowestoft Cemetery so he could take flowers to the graves of his wife and his son, William, who had been killed in an accident when he was a boy.

I was alone with my grandfather when he died, having been confined to bed for some time. A nurse had been in to see him and I was sitting reading in his room when he alarmed me with the noise he began making and I quickly called my mother who explained to me that Granfer had passed away. I thought the world of the old man and was very proud of him.

Watling's Yard, Clapham Road, opposite Surrey Street, where I was put in a barrel for cheeking the foreman.

George, Kenneth and I. Sadly my little brother Kenny died shortly after my fourth birthday from eating the poisonous part of a crab. Mother said that she had cleaned the crab but Kenny wandered down the yard, rummaged in the dustbin and ate the 'dead man's fingers'.

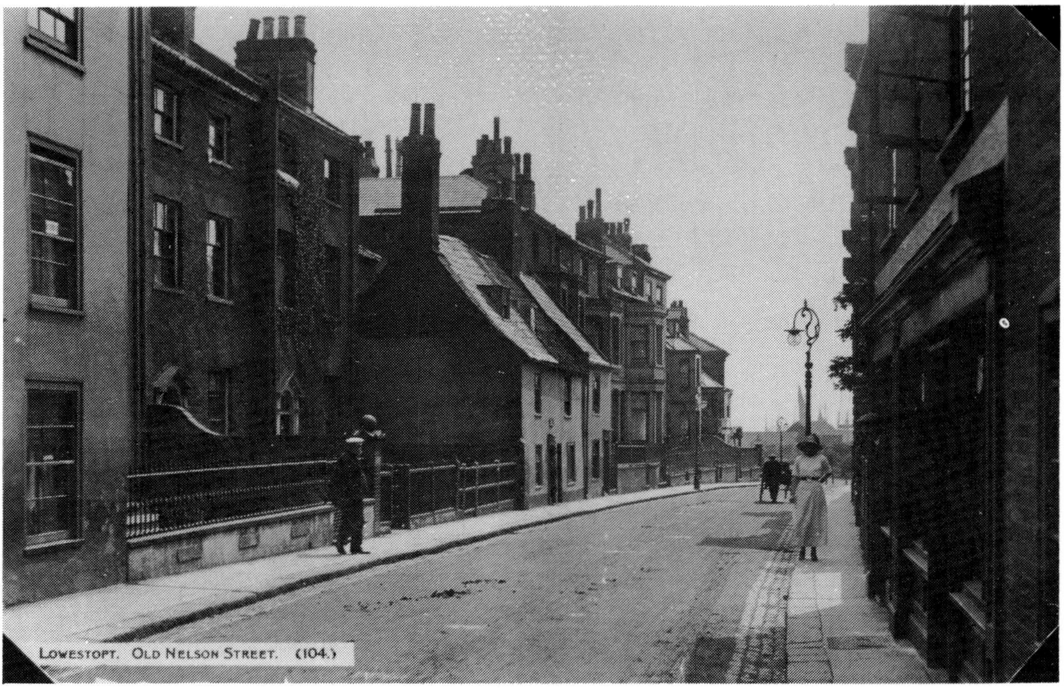

Old Nelson Street, where we lived during the 1930s, was attacked by German bombers three times and none of these buildings are standing today.

A Thirties Childhood

It is difficult to convey to people who did not grow up in pre-war days the community spirit that existed then that makes us sometimes think of them as the 'good old days'. No doubt life today is much more comfortable but those of us who remember the 1930s remember good neighbours, helping one another; people sharing what little possessions they had and genuinely caring one for another. We remember small, family-owned corner shops, where goods were sold loose and weighed out by the ounce if necessary.

I remember the days when good manners were considered important and a child knew his place and benefitted from the security of discipline. We didn't have many clothes and unless you were the oldest in the family, what you did have were hand-me downs, we didn't have many toys — we invented games in streets that were virtually traffic-free, our meals would not be recognised as food by today's children, but we did have a sense of belonging, we had large families who kept in touch with one another, we could walk around in safety and play in the open-air on grassland and beaches.

Looking back you realize just how hard times were then; the working class were poor, and I mean poor. People lived in dread of debt and the hated workhouse. On a couple of occasions there was no food in the house at all and coming home from school and seeing my mother crying because there was nothing to eat in the house is something that I never forgot. It is imprinted on my mind for life.

In the 1930s there was no social security and anyone asking for help was subjected to a 'means test'. An officer came to the home to assess the need and anyone owning such things as a chest-of-drawers, a piano or a gramophone would be refused help on the grounds that they could sell their 'luxuries'. All they said that you needed were chairs to sit on, a table to eat from and a bed to sleep in. A lot of men applying for relief would be sent to Oulton workhouse, known locally as 'the Spike', to do a day's work for a meal ticket which could then be exchanged for food at a shop.

Every possible economy was made. I remember my mother saving the little pieces of left-over soap every week and when she had enough, soaking them in hot water and moulding them all together for use on wash-day. A regular Saturday night job was to cut newspapers into squares to be strung up for use in the toilet which was outside the house as was common in those days.

In Stanley Street at this time was Mr Bell's Bakery situated where is now Boggis the butchers shop. I recall many times Mother making a cake and sending us boys to Bell's with it to have it baked for a penny or tuppence. The purpose of this was to save money on the cost of fuel at home. Some people used to have their whole meals cooked this way years ago, but I can only remember taking cakes.

Oulton Workhouse, known locally as the 'Spike'. The prospect of being sent there terrified people; now Lothingland Hospital.

Norton's premises in London Road North have now been incorporated into the Trustees Savings Bank. The old TSB replaced Buck's sweet shop. Coming through the alleyway opposite one day when I was a child I was so excited by the display of chocolate eggs in the window of Buck's that I dashed across the road without looking, was hit by a heavy old trade-bike and ended up in hospital.

Roman Hill Infants School in Beckham Road and the Junior School in Roman Road. At the time of writing these schools, which I attended, are being demolished.

Often we were sent to the bakers for stale pastries, these being the cakes not sold — the left-overs. For two or three pence you could get a bag full of them. The butcher supplied us with two penny-worth of bones which were boiled for stews, ham bones being boiled up with split peas and a swede to make pea soup. We also asked for pigs' trotters, or even a sheep's head which could be made into a sheep's head stew!

Bobbins the butcher whose shop was on the corner of Milton Road and Clapham Road always kept a supply of small pork cheeses under the counter for the children who called in to get their mother's order and fruiterers supplied many families with 'spotted' fruit, such as apples, oranges and bananas for a few pence. This was mostly done last thing on a Saturday night at the Triangle Plain just before the market closed.

Sometimes we'd have fish and chips. The orders were mostly for 'one and one' — a penny-worth of chips and a penny fish. If the bloke in the fish shop liked the look of your face then occasionally he'd throw in a few extra chips or sometimes even an extra fish.

My favourite at tea-time was a condensed milk sandwich with a little sugar sprinkled on for a special treat. Dripping sandwiches were also popular. Stale bread was not wasted, it was toasted or made into milk-sop or bread puddings. Another favourite was 'bread and currant' pudding which consisted of stale bread being mixed with currants and covered in hot milk.

What we called 'damps' could be purchased from the sweet shop. Sweets weren't pre-wrapped then and some would become sticky and congealed together — the kids used to love them. Another favourite was broken biscuits, a mixture of all the broken pieces out of the glass-topped tins that biscuits were sold from then.

Once or twice a week we children used to go down to the fish market to scrounge a cod's head. Mother would boil this and the flesh, mixed with boiled potatoes or swedes, would make a meal for the whole family.

Despite the privations life at home was happy but my schooldays were not altogether so and I soon discovered that one or two very strict teachers could make a child's life very nerve-racking although when I first started school at Roman Hill Infants in Beckham Road, (later than I should have done due to an unfortunate accident) the Head was a lovely woman by the name of Miss Mills.

When we were old enough we were moved to Roman Hill Junior School, which was really part of the same school but facing into Roman Road. From there I went to Church Road School (later known as St Margaret's, but now sadly demolished) where the Head-teacher was a Mrs Rice. I was put into Miss Newby's class and found school life none too pleasant, but I eventually settled down although whenever I could I would take time off from school for the least little thing.

On Sport's Day we were marched to St Peter's Street playing field, which is now Lowestoft College Campus or were taken to Corton Road playing field (now the site of a housing development) but which at that time stood away from the houses close to the site of the old railway station.

My favourite lesson was swimming and I was never happier than when it was time to go to the old Lowestoft Swimming Pool on the North Denes (now a caravan site) for swimming lessons. This was about the only 'subject' that I was good at and I eventually represented Church Road School, and later Roman Hill School, against other schools in the district.

I did not make the grade to reach higher schools like the Secondary School in Yarmouth Road (now the Denes High) or the Central School in Herring Fishery Score so it was to Roman Hill Senior Boys School that I was sent. This school had the reputation of being a very tough one with an equally tough Headmaster called Mr Bleby. I found out later that he was a South African who at one time had been in charge of a Borstal Institution but certainly his discipline stood us in good stead when we later entered the Forces.

When we were marched from our classrooms to the main hall for assembly quietness was the order of the day. Once inside no one dared breathe, let alone talk or make a sound, for fear of Mr Bleby's wrath. When we lined up to go into our classrooms he had a habit of appearing from nowhere and would start firing questions, "What is eight times eight?" . . . "What is nine times nine?" and so on. The only trouble was that he never gave anyone time to answer the questions!

Most mornings there would be a prefect on the school gate who would take your name if you were late. Arriving late once or twice was usually dealt with with a caution, but those who were late more than three times in a week were called up onto the stage at the Friday morning assembly where Mr Bleby would be standing, cane in hand and told to hold out their hands, promptly receiving two or three strokes of the cane on each. If you did not hold your hand high enough then the cane would come swishing upwards until it was at the right height. If you knew that you were in for a caning an onion cut in half and rubbed over the palms of the hands was said to take out the sting, but I'm afraid it never seemed to work for me!

Once a week we would walk down to the school garden under the guidance of Mr Brown the gardening teacher. The gardens were situated in Avondale Road where today the small buildings belonging to Lowestoft College stand. They were surrounded by four high bricks walls and a large wooden gate. On one occasion Mr Brown told us to dig shallow trenches in which to plant potatoes. He then left us while he returned to school for a short while. We all got stuck in but two of the lads, Jimmy Neave and Ronnie Clarke got carried away with their digging and when Mr Brown returned all you could see above ground level were the tops of their heads. 'Old Brownie' as he was known called them out of the trench and asked them in the sarcastic tones which only teachers seem to have perfected, what size of potatoes they intended planting? Jimmy and Ronnie stood there with bowed heads, shuffling their feet and mumbling, "We don't know," expecting Old Brownie's wrath to descend upon them any second. Instead, he amazed everyone by saying, "Well done lads, we needed a compost ditch and now you lads have dug us one."

Out of school I belonged to a number of youth organisations. Early on I went to the Methodist Church Sunday School opposite Gordon Road (now Courts furnishing shop) and it was here that I joined the Life Boys under Henry Sparham and Harry Chamberlain. Later on I changed and went to Christ Church at the bottom of Herring Fishery Score. Here I became a member of the 'Young Harvesters' which was held in a room above the Church Hall. When I was a bit older I joined the Boy's Brigade at Christ Church. By the time of the outbreak of war I was in the Navy League Sea Cadet Corps.

The bottom end of Old Nelson Street in the late 1950s. Part of the Misses Bishops' sweet-shop where I worked after school can be seen on the corner.

Horace Bishop's greengrocery in Duke's Head Street, one of the shops for which I ran errands.

John Bishop's shop in London Road North (now Cook's furnishers) where I worked out of school hours delivering paraffin and running orders around.

The old Lowestoft Swimming Pool. I loved swimming and eventually represented Church Road and Roman Hill Schools and later the army. I was useless at every other sport.

Herring Fishery Score also known as Christ Church Score. The back way to our house in Old Nelson Street was just behind the telegraph pole. The left-hand side is now Lowestoft Police Station. On the right was the Central School and at the bottom Christ Church Hall.

Work and Play

To help Mother I did various jobs in between school hours, working at local shops or doing paper-rounds. My first big job, as I called it, was working for Billy Pye who lived half-way down Old Nelson Street. He had a pony and trap and we used to go round delivering newspapers to the outlying villages which took up all of a Sunday morning from eight o'clock. The pony was known as Tommy and was stabled at the back of Edwards in the High Street, just at the rear of the Old Central School, where at that time (the 1930s) there was a row of cottages. Every Sunday morning I would go and meet Billy at his home where he and his wife used to sort out the papers. When they were ready we would put the bags of papers in the trap, climb up, and head out of town to deliver them. Our travels took us to Corton, Hopton, Blundeston, Lound and Oulton Village. We would then finish up back at Lowestoft where I would be paid half-a-crown.

One weekday the pony had lashed-out and broken Billy Pye's leg so I was asked to take the pony and trap out alone so that he didn't lose his income. I agreed to do so knowing full well that his livelihood depended on it, but I must admit, being only about twelve years of age, I was dead scared! Anyway we got away all right and I began to feel more confident. We stopped outside the *Village Maid* at Lound to deliver the papers, but when I tried to get going again old Tommy just would not budge; it was hopeless. I stood there crying when a man came up and asked me what was wrong. When I told him the pony would not move he went into the pub and must have told the landlord, because he came out carrying a pint mug.

"This is what he wants," he said, giving Tommy a drink.

"Can I pay you next week when I come again?" I asked, "you know I daren't spend any of Billy's money."

"It's OK," he laughed, adding, "You know what to do next time he won't move, old son!"

All went well until we arrived at the Blundeston *Plough* where I had to explain to the landlord about the pint of beer as I was under-age to buy it. The landlord was understanding and I think he felt sorry for a twelve year-old. The only trouble was that I had to explain everything to the landlords of the Oulton *Red House* and the *White Hart* at Hopton, who all helped and trusted me for the money to be paid the following week. I stuck the job until Billy got well, then I left, having had a few worrying Sundays!

On weekdays after school I worked for John Bishop who had an ironmongers shop in London Road North. I ran errands for him and delivered goods and paraffin on his trade-bike for sixpence a week. When he was not busy I would nip down to see his two sisters who had a sweet-shop at the corner of Old Nelson Street and Whapload Road. His brother Tom Bishop had a fishing store next door but I never did any work for him. Another brother I helped and ran about for was Horace Bishop who had a fruit shop in Dukes Head Street. When I finished errands for this good, and I emphasise *good*, family, I would return to John Bishop's where his sister, I think her name was Becky, would read me a verse from the Bible, but I'm afraid it did me little good.

From there I went to work, in between school hours again, for Mr Meridan Smith. He and his mother had the sweet-shop called 'Ye Mecca' in the High Street (now Pandoras Inspirations). Mr Smith also owned Francis' Fruit Shop three or four doors away (now 'Sizzers' the hair-dressers). I was an errand boy cum shop assistant and sometimes, being always hungry, I used to have a crafty eat of an apple, banana or orange but this came to an end when I made the mistake of leaving the peel on top of the rubbish in the dustbin. Of course, when the lid was lifted my crime was exposed!

I eventually left the employ of Meridan Smith and went as a paper-boy at Button's the newsagent and tobacconist in the High Street (opposite what was then the London Drapery stores and is now Harrod's carpet shop). To earn a little bit more money I walked a neighbour's dog for which I was paid sixpence a week.

With some of this hard-earned money we kids could treat ourselves to some of life's little luxuries. Even for a farthing you could buy sweets and how we loved to go to a sweet-shop and choose from bulls-eyes, pear drops, acid drops, aniseed balls, liquorice in many shapes and sizes, tiger nuts, locusts — the choice seemed endless and all for a ha'penny an ounce. There were love-hearts with messages printed on them, toffee in slabs and broken into pieces with a hammer, sherbet dabs and cachous, and because they were weighed out loose and not pre-packed sweet-shops had an aroma all their own.

We could also get our comics, and there were scores of them to pick from. *Chips, Film Fun, Chick's Own, Razzler, Dazzle, Tiger Tim, Billy Bunter, Hotspur, Wizard, Rover* to name but a few that come quickly to mind, each a penny or tuppence.

During the school holidays I went long-shoring for shrimps and sprats with my grandfather, old Mike Rose. This was always fun even though it meant a bit of hard work pulling the trawl aboard and sorting out the shrimps from the crabs and weeds. Granfer always had a fork handy so that he could stick it into the small, poisonous weever fish and flick them overboard. A sting from one of these was very painful. I have known my father, when he was pricked by a weever, to wash his hand in paraffin and then hold it over the fire so that the heat would take the sting out.

When I was not wanted by my grandfather or anybody else then I would be given a bottle of lemonade (made from lemonade powder) and some sandwiches and sent out for the day, either to the beach or Denes. Sometimes our trips to the beach took us to a spot by the 'Old Extension' which we called Jackson's Corner. Swimming costumes were not needed for it was just a case of stripping-off and running into the water — boys and girls sometimes — it made no difference. Doing this day after day we soon became good swimmers.

The Life Boys, outside the United Methodist Church in London Road North. I am seated front left. The Church was demolished and Courts now occupy the site.

The Old Extension, Jackson's Corner, where we used to swim. All the land area is now covered by SLP.

In Jackson's corner was a shingle mill and a crane for dragging out the shingle from the sea bed. This made a deep hole and this was our favourite place for swimming. Some of the older, more daring boys would climb to the top of the crane and dive off into the water which took some nerve.

If we did not go swimming then the harbour beach became our playground. We would often walk round to the fish market and scrounge an old fish head or fish skeleton. We would tie this to a piece of twine and use it for 'crabbing' (catching crabs) either on the Hamilton Dock or the Old Extension. Most of the crabs we caught were thrown back. Sometimes we would make a fishing line from a hook, a piece of string and an old net cork. Bait was a bit of herring, crab, or even a smashed mussel or limpet.

Sometimes when we were playing on the harbour beach we would pick up a net cork, flat or round; then out would come our shut-knives and we would shape the cork into a boat complete with mast and paper sails. We would spend hours watching our craft floating across the dock, sometimes throwing stones into the water to try and get them to splash just behind our boat to make it go further.

As children we were always getting into mischief, and our disagreements were usually settled with the fist. When we were kids at the Beach we used to look up to the older boys if we encountered any troubles and I always looked up to two lads named Jackie McCarthy and Gus Jensen. Jackie and I parted company in 1939 and we didn't meet again until 1987 when we had a reunion at Gus's house, reminiscing over old times.

Every area of the town had its 'gang'. There was the Beach Gang, the Brickfield Gang, the Mariner's Street Gang and the Long Row Gang from Cathcart Street. I was in the 'Beach Gang' and we used to meet in the cellar of a big old wooden house in Frost's Alley Score.

Occasionally we used to get a puff of a fag, but what we usually smoked as boys was basket cane. We would go to old Jasper Day, who made all the herring baskets, and get a handful of his snippings, put them in our pockets and then go and buy a ha'penny box of matches and light up. We used to go down on the harbour beach and puff on this old cane, but it tasted really vile.

We often used to make rafts to sail into the harbour from the Old Extension or sometimes, better still, we would find an old painter's raft or punt which we would use. Like all kids we did not seem to know the meaning of fear and often we would climb right along to the end of the Old Extension with the sea breaking over us – it was a case of hanging on for dear life! I can also remember when we used to go up to Belle Vue Park and dare each other to walk across the old Jubilee Bridge on the hand-rail! When we got to the other end we would jump off on to the bank – another daft thing to do! When I was a child there was not much traffic, except for horses and carts, and something that we often did was to run behind a cart, hanging on with our legs dangling. When the carter realized what was going on we had to jump off quickly to avoid a whip across the fingers!

Sometimes we went to Mr Durrant the fruiterer for old sacks. These would be unstitched and opened out, then with a sailmaker's needle and some twine they would be sewn together to make a tent. Broom handles would then disappear from one or two homes and we would all make our way to the Denes or the waste ground at the back of the old gas works to go camping. This was all right when it was fine weather but there were times when we returned home soaking wet and miserable. Another favourite playing ground was the waste ground at the back of the fish market along by Battery Green Road where the ice factory and garage now stand. Here were stacked thousands of empty fish boxes and we used to move the boxes around and build ourselves dens. These 'dens' also served as great hideaways that would could nip into if the law appeared.

Some of the other places we played included Normanston Park, Nicholas Everitt Park and Kirkley Fen. There were no television sets when we were children so after school or at weekends we made our own enjoyment and invented games to play. Other games had been played by our parents and their parents before them, some no doubt are still being played today. In those days we used to wander for miles looking for, and finding, our own amusement.

Often when we came off the Beach we used to walk to the back of the *Clapham Hotel* and pinch the empty bottles that were kept there. We then took them in the 'Jug and Smoke' room where the landlord bought them back! This was one way of getting our picture money. Eventually the landlord found out what was going on and marked the empties and that was the end of that. Sometimes, if we only had a few pennies between us and wanted to go to the pictures, one of us would pay the tuppence and go in. After he'd been in a few minutes he'd go to the toilet, open the window and let the rest of us in. As soon as that window went up we were over the wall like a load of rabbits. About twelve of us would get in for tuppence!

We had plenty of cinemas to go to. As I remember, starting from south of the bridge there was the *Grand*, *Playhouse*, *Palace*, *Hippodrome*, *Coronet*, *Odeon*, *Marina*, *Regent Alfresco* and the *Cosy Corner* – later re-named the *Regent* but always known affectionately by everyone as the 'Flea-pit' or the 'Bug-house', because once you got in there you'd really be on the itch! In Norwich Road there was also the *Ideal* Cinema converted from an old chapel about 1937. Two other cinemas I have been told of but do not remember were the *Public Hall* and *Pakefield* Cinema in St Georges Road, Pakefield.

May Day was a good day for us because this was when we went round the houses collecting money, singing:

Climbing up the walls, knocking down the spiders
Cabbages and turnips too.
Put them in your alley alley saucepan
Then we'll have a rare old stew.

We would dress up in adults' clothes, blacken our faces, and of course we had our 'May Queen'. No-one I have spoken to seems to know the origin of the little ditty or how it came about but after some research I discovered that it is to do with the Salvation Army. I am informed that somewhere in Suffolk, in the Woodbridge area, two young Salvation Army lasses used to go around the streets – one banging a big drum and the other one shouting out the Gospel. After a while they managed to get an old wooden building to use as a soup kitchen. It was while volunteers were cleaning the place up that the words originated. While they were up the steps dusting and knocking down the cobwebs one of the lasses started singing, "Climbing up the wall, knocking down the spiders". Soon other words were added; the 'cabbages and turnips' refer to the vegetables that were laying about waiting to be put into the soup, the 'alley alley saucepan' could be derived from the fact that the saucepan in which the soup was prepared had been scrounged from one of the back-alleys in the neighbourhood – after all, as I have said, saucepans and frying-pans used to hang on the walls in backyards in those days!

Firework Day was another special day. For weeks beforehand we would wheel our home-made guys around the town for the odd coin or two with which to buy fireworks. A lot of pride went into the making of a 'guy' and they were not like those that children make these days. A pair of trousers and a shirt would be stuffed with straw, as were the arms of a jacket fitted over the stuffed shirt. Onto the legs went rubber boots. The face was a mop covered in rags with a piece of white cloth for the face. The eyes were two Catherine Wheels, the nose was a Sparkling Pyramid point outwards, and the mouth was a Jumping Jack, all stitched in place. On the head was placed a flat cap or trilby.

These guys all finished up on top of the local bonfire just before it was lit. The bonfires were big and could be found scattered on open spaces all over the town. They were built by all the children of a neighbourhood in the weeks preceding the 5th November and it was a matter of local honour and pride to have the biggest and best bonfire. People would walk all over the place to admire and compare the different bonfires. It was great fun and the communal building of the bonfire reflected a community spirit which today seems to have all but disappeared.

However, life was soon to change. War clouds started to darken the sky, with the press writing about Nazi Germany and the atrocities to the Jews, and we heard of the refugees fleeing to England for safety. Then came that fateful day – September 3rd, 1939 – when war was declared. It was not many minutes after the declaration that the air raid sirens sounded. That was our first experience of running to an air raid shelter, wondering what to expect. It was a false alarm but later, when the bombs did start to drop, we were to find out and then real fear came into our lives.

The opening of the *Ideal* Cinema, Norwich Road in the 1930s, above and the *Palace* Cinema when the front faced London Road South, below.

It was in streets like these that we played, untroubled by traffic. We played football and cricket, tops and whips, jack-stones and hop-scotch. We swapped cigarette-cards and bowled hoops that we got from the cooper's yard. We also played 'glass-alleys'. I see that what we called 'glass-alleys' the children now call 'marbles', which when I was a child were little round balls made of hard clay and painted.

Christ Church Square. The tall building (top centre) was London Drapery Stores where I worked as an errand boy. The bay window belonged to Edward's and it was at the rear of this building that Mr Pye stabled his pony, Tommy.

Spurgeon Street, one of the many little streets in the 'Beach Village'.

Triangle Plain. Before the war all the townsfolk flocked here on a Saturday night to buy goods at reduced prices. Note the RAC road sign and 'Dr Who' type police box.

Roman Hill Senior Boys School in the 1930s. Mr Bleby, the head, is standing on the right.

The War Years

Lowestoft was made a naval base — the headquarters being Sparrow's Nest, the name of which in true naval tradition was changed to *HMS Europa.* Big hotels and public buildings were commandeered to be used as billets for the forces coming to Lowestoft. Lorries full of sailors could be seen travelling around the town, stopping every so often to drop them off at private houses where they were to be billeted.

Fishing boats became mine-sweepers and the main industry of Lowestoft came to a halt. Those boats not commandeered for the war-effort left the town to fish from Fleetwood, Milford Haven and other safer ports where fishing was still allowed.

I was getting on for fourteen years old when the war started and like many other boys of my age I felt excited — we were going to war! Little did I realise then the horror and tragedy that the war was going to bring. This attitude was reflected in our school work. For the first few months everything was war. When we were doing art work all the children were drawing tanks, planes, fighting, bombing — anything to do with the war. I can remember our art teacher, Mrs Bird, saying, "Why war pictures, why not something else?" Naturally we thought England was just going to knock the Germans cold in a matter of a few months!

In the course of our lessons we were taught how to proceed to the air raid shelters and how to put on a gas mask but most of our information and advice came from the wireless, newspapers and from leaflets and pamphlets put through our doors.

Notice came that evacuation of the town was to take place and those that could were asked to leave Lowestoft. Many did and were followed by some of the shop-keepers who, realising that their trade was going, also packed their bags and left. One day all of us school-children took a note home advising our parents that if they wanted their children evacuated to a safer part of the country they should sign the attached form and return it. This was voluntary — no one would be forced to go.

I went home with my note and played-up because I wanted to go away with my friends. In the end Mother gave way and let me go because I was so insistent but I was the only one of our family evacuated. When the day to go finally came, June 2nd, 1940, I packed my suitcase — a towel, change of clothes, tooth-brush and all that sort of thing — and with my gas-mask in its case hanging round my neck and label tied to my collar I went to Roman Hill Senior Boys' School where I was a pupil, jumped on the bus and away I went to the railway station; the start of a long journey to the Midlands. My destination was a village called Clowne in Derbyshire. Other schools went to Worksop, Creswell, Bolsover, Matlock and Langwith and the population of Lowestoft fell to 22,000.

SPECIAL SUNDAY EDITION

ARNOLDS
HEAVY BLUE CLOTH
2/6
GT. YARMOUTH

Eastern Evening News

NO RISE IN PRICES YET
Lancaster Cloth
Dark Blind Hollands
Black Italian
All at USUAL PRICES
AT
BONDS, NORWICH

NORWICH, SUNDAY, SEPTEMBER 3, 1939 ONE PENNY

WAR WITH GERMANY

Momentous Broadcast by the Premier

BRITAIN'S ULTIMATUM EXPIRED AT 11 a.m. TO-DAY

"We have a clear conscience"

RESOLVED TO FINISH AN INTOLERABLE POSITION

Fighting Brute Force and Bad Faith

BRITAIN BECAME AT WAR WITH GERMANY AT 11 a.m. TO-DAY. HER ULTIMATUM TO THE GERMAN

The Prime Minister snapped outside No. 10, Downing Street.

Premier's Statement To Commons

NO GERMAN REPLY TO LAST WARNING

"We are ready"

MEMBERS ROSE AND CHEERED WHEN THE PREMIER ENTERED THE HOUSE OF COMMONS TO-DAY TO MAKE THE ANNOUNCEMENT THAT THIS COUNTRY WAS AT WAR WITH GERMANY.

The Premier said, "When I spoke last night in the House I could not but be aware that in some part of the House there were doubts and some bewilderment as to whether there had been any hesitation or vacillation on the part of the Government.

"We were in consultation all day

FRENCH ULTIMATUM EXPIRES AT 5 P.M.

PARIS, Sunday.

FRANCE TO-DAY DELIVERED AN ULTIMATUM TO GERMANY DEMANDING THAT GERMAN TROOPS WITHDRAW FROM POLAND. THE ULTIMATUM EXPIRES AT 5 P.M. (B.S.T.).

LATE NEWS
(SEE ALSO BACK PAGE)

How the *Eastern Evening News* announced the outbreak of the Second World War.

When we finally arrived, tired and weary, we were taken in groups around the streets of Clowne with a guide knocking on doors asking if they were still willing to take in evacuees. I remember hanging back until the very last, and an elderly lady coming to her door. There was me sitting on a suitcase, fed-up and wishing I had not been so keen to leave home! The lady must have taken pity on me because I was asked in even though she was not officially listed to take evacuees.

For the next month this was to be my home, 58 Boughton Lane, Clowne; Mr and Mrs Edwards were my foster-parents and although I could never have had a better foster-mother, my adventure turned out to be more of a nightmare and I was fed-up and unhappy. I missed my family and my home town dreadfully and my mother knew this from my letters.

On my second day there, Mrs Edwards said to me, "Why don't you go out and play down on the rec?"

This sounded just my cup of tea and I eagerly asked her where it was, and in a short while I was wandering off following her directions. I could find no sign of the 'wreck' she had spoken of and so I asked a man.

He said, "Look over there – you can see the slide and swings." I said, "I know but where's the wreck?" Then the penny dropped.

"You're a 'vac aren't you?" he said, "You mean the wreck of a ship, we mean recreation park."

When I told Mrs Edwards she laughed and asked where I had hoped to find a shipwreck in the middle of Derbyshire.

One Sunday morning, about a month after my arrival, I was standing by Mrs Edwards' front gate when a car drew up outside and a man I seemed to recognise got out. He came over and spoke to me, "Do you know where Jack Rose lives?" he asked.

I said, "I'm Jack Rose!"

"Well," he said, "I've come to take you back home."

Tears welled-up in my eyes and I flew indoors crying, "Mrs Edwards! There's a man come to take me home!"

She helped me to pack and as we said goodbye I could see a tear or two in her eyes. Once we were in the car and on the way home I was full of joy. The man who had come for me was Mr Gardiner, a Lowestoft window-cleaner, but why Mother had fetched me home I wasn't sure. On the way we were stopped several times by soldiers but Mr Gardiner passed me off as his son.

Eventually we were back in territory that was only too familiar to me and once again I was back in Lowestoft outside my own front door. I knocked and walked in to be greeted with tears and kisses. I was back home with my family. My mother's first words told me the reason I had been fetched home. She said, "The bombs have started to come. If we die we all die as a family." The bombing of Lowestoft had started although I had missed the first raid of the war while I was evacuated.

Understandably the air-raids frightened Mother and because at this time we had an air-raid shelter which was too damp to sleep in every night we all went to my cousin's

My first job after returning from evacuation was at Billy Cooper's, the naval tailor, in the High Street. The site is now occupied by the veterinary practice.

Lowestoft Steam Laundry, Whapload Road. I worked here as a van boy in 1940 for nine shillings and sixpence a week, frequently from eight in the morning until seven in the evening.

house at 101 Oulton Road, which was then on the outskirts of the town, where she hoped we'd be safer. My aunt lived in one of a pair of cottages near the *Norman Warrior* public house. The cottage was surrounded by fields in those days. Even here we weren't particularly safe, in fact you weren't safe anywhere for bombs fell everywhere and anywhere, on one occasion in Woods Loke not far from my aunt's house where we were all sheltering! Close by in St. Margaret's fields, there was a big battery of anti-aircraft guns and searchlights and during a raid when they opened up the whole house used to shake to the regular boom! boom! boom! boom! of the guns. The searchlights lit up the sky and sometimes German planes would fly down the beams and machine-gun the lights.

Now that I was back home and there was no school I was at a loose end and didn't know what to do. Mother soon made up my mind for me. "You're not going to run the streets," she told me, "you'll get a job." So I left school when I was fourteen and got a job at Billy Cooper's, the naval tailor, in the High Street opposite the *Royal Falcon*. I was employed as a shop assistant and errand boy with a starting wage of five shillings and six pence a week, and a promise of seven shillings and sixpence after a month if I was any good.

As the sailors came in for new uniforms I measured them. They each had an allotment form to be completed so that so much would be deducted from their wages each week. When I was not measuring for uniforms I was riding round the town on a bike delivering the finished uniforms to the various naval bases.

One day while I was in the fitting-room measuring up a sailor for his uniform, I looked through the small peep-hole in the wall through which we could keep an eye on the shop, and I saw the new shop-assistant take a pound note from the till and put it in his pocket. I didn't know what to do, so I told Mother when I got home. She said to me, "When you get back you give in your notice." She obviously didn't want me to become involved in anything like that. I did as she said, telling my boss, Mr. Gudrum, that I was leaving because I wanted a better job. I was disappointed at having to leave because I was very happy there.

My next job was at the Lowestoft Steam Laundry in Whapload Road, the manageress being Mrs Metcalf. Here I signed on as a van boy to work with Mr Chadwick the driver. We had an old green bus with boarded-up windows and my job was to collect and deliver the laundry in town and also in the villages as far away as Southwold and Walberswick. My wage was nine shillings and sixpence a week.

One day Mr Chadwick told me that he had asked for a pay rise for me and wanted to know if I had got it. I said I hadn't. "Right," he replied, "You come with me." He took me to the Union Office in Suffolk Road and after speaking to an old boy by the name of Matthews, I joined the union. I didn't really know what was going on but three weeks later I was called into the office at the laundry and given £25, a back payment. Apparently as I was still classed as a minor I had been working excessive hours. When I was in the office I was asked why I had not said I was in the union when I took the job. I said that I had not been asked and anyway I had joined the union after signing on. Then I was cross-examined as to all the whys and wherefores of how I had come to join the union.

By now I was getting hot-tempered with all the questions and not wanting to involve Mr Chadwick I said, "You can stick your job. I am giving my notice!" With that I turned my back and walked out. At the end of the week when I went to collect my wages I was asked to reconsider but I was adamant about leaving. Later, when I arrived home and put the £25 in my mother's hand the joy on her face made it all worthwhile. I would have worked twenty-four hours a day for her.

Because of the war, with the men being called up and going away, there was always plenty of work to be had. My next job after the laundry was as an errand boy at the London Drapery Stores (now Harrod's carpet shop) in the High Street. The manager here was a Londoner, a Mr. Vokes. My duties entailed delivering orders and doing odd-jobs around the shop. I had to sweep and polish the floors (using a polish that I made myself by melting beeswax on a paraffin stove and adding a few drops of turps — the mixture was then left to set). Other duties included cleaning and maintaining the boiler down in the basement, polishing the brass-work round the windows and also putting up the black-out all around the building. This was an important job because if it was not done correctly and light showed you could be fined.

While I was employed there I helped convert the coal-cellar under the front of the shop into an air-raid shelter by strengthening the roof, lime-washing it all out and fitting bunk beds. At night, if the air-raid warning sounded, people from opposite would come over and share it with us. There were Mr and Mrs Saunders from the butcher's shop; the Misses Cathpole from the cake shop, and Mr and Mrs Button the news-agents. I don't know how we'd have got on if we had been bombed because there was a gas-pipe running right through the cellar level with the ceiling, and it wasn't the easiest place to evacuate!

The girls who worked at the London Drapery Stores were all friendly and helpful and I had a favourite, Mabel Chamberlain. The other girls I recall were Miss Clarke, Miss Baldry, Miss Boughtell, Miss Brookes, Miss Tuddenham, Miss Mitchell, Miss Pratt, Miss Chapman, Miss Martell and Queenie Lark. At night they would work in relays to do a firewatching duty. I remember one day cycling to Yarmouth Town Hall on a trade bike to fetch their special helmets which they had to wear while fire-watching. I went as quickly as I could and came back during an air-raid but all the manager said was, "Been a while, haven't you?"

The job I dreaded the most was taking rolls of lino to South Lowestoft. I used to strap them across the handle bars of my bike which made it look like an aeroplane! My main dread was coming to the bridge because nine times out of ten I would be stopped by a policeman. Out would come his tape measure and he would check to see that they were no longer than six feet. I must admit that it was dangerous carrying the lino like that especially as I could have caught on to something, but it was the only way to deliver it.

On the night of 22nd July, 1941, while we were still making our nightly visits to Oulton Broad, my Granny, her sister and her sister's twin daughters were killed in the dreadful bombing raid that flattened St Leonard's Road. I've been told that a bomb went straight through their house and hit the Morrison table shelter in which they all lay huddled for protection. They didn't stand a chance and only bits and pieces were ever found. I can clearly remember the morning after that raid. I was getting ready for work at the time and my mother's sister who lived near St Leonard's Road came to

The St Leonard's Road air-raid, 1941, in which my grandmother, her sister and her sister's twin daughters were killed.

The 'Anderson' air-raid shelter, named after the Home Secretary of the day. By 1940, 2,300,000 Andersons had been produced, sufficient to protect 12,500,000 people. They were six feet high and four-feet six inches wide by six feet six inches long and were designed to withstand the blast from a 500 pound bomb falling twenty feet away.

break the sad news. She had walked and run all the way from Kirkley. We were devastated and heart-broken and I cried all the way to work. I often wondered how my aunt must have felt when she emerged from her own shelter and saw her mother's house flattened.

After several months at the London Drapery I got fed-up and gave my notice. I was asked to reconsider, with the promise that I would be trained as a manager, but I declined and left. I felt I wanted to do something more permanent.

After finishing there I went to the Youth Employment Office, which at that time was in Gordon Road, to find another job. I was given a card and told to wait outside the railway station to be picked up by a truck and taken to Ellough to work on the airfield which was under construction there. When we got there I queued up with a lot of men outside a large wooden shed. On entering, the chap behind the desk remarked, "Hello, they're sending us schoolboys now!" On being told that I was too young for the kind of work offered, I left the shed and forgetting there was transport, starting to make my way back to Lowestoft by trying to hitch a lift. After walking for nearly two miles I was picked up by a gentleman in a car who dropped me off at a bus stop and wished me well.

Eventually I got a job with 'Rooney' Pearson, a builder. Then one day, a few weeks later, I happened to bump into Sidney Pearce, a pal of mine, who was working for Stan Button the builder in Raglan Street. Sid said a labourer was needed so away I went and got the job. The business was only a small family concern, but it paid fifteen shillings and sixpence a week for a start! The employees were Sid Pearce, 'Gee' Davies, Leslie Dennington, Sid Runacres, Mr Sims, Harry Skillings Sr and Harry Skillings Jr. Later Brian Field came and joined us.

I was put with Harry Skillings Senior as his labourer. He was a hard task-master and there were several who would not work with him but he knew his job. Despite numerous rows with him I stuck it out because I respected the work he did – he was a craftsman. Among the jobs he taught me was how to make lime putty and horse-hair mortar. This knowledge came in handy as being able to do this saved me from losing money when the other men were sent home on wet days.

Naturally, being in the building trade, most of the work I did consisted of repairing bomb damage after the raids on the town. I replaced slates and tiles, repaired down-pipes and drains and mended ceilings. For this I'd knock out the old plaster and then nail large cardboard panels to the rafters. Splines would be put across to hide the joins and then the painter came and painted the cardboard white and the splines brown – proper old wartime ceilings they were. Over ninety per cent of my work consisted of repairing war damage.

I was often on a roof during a raid and afterwards, among the *débris*, I picked up watches, false teeth, bits of bodies and even on one occasion half a hand! Believe it or not this was classed as essential war work and when London was being blitzed they sent people from Lowestoft to help clear up. My boss got me exempted as I was working for a small firm that could not afford to lose the manpower. I did try to volunteer for the Forces but discovered that I was classed as a reserve worker and had to wait until I was a bit older than eighteen to be called-up.

By the middle of 1941 we had the use of an Anderson shelter in Herring Fishery

Score which we shared with the family who lived at the *Spread Eagle* pub (now the *Wheatsheaf*). This was installed, with two or three others, on a piece of land over the wall at the bottom of our garden. I remember helping Dad to build wooden bunk-beds to put in it. We never used it much for it was very damp and smelly – Mother was particularly loathe to use it and eventually, early in 1942 when Mother became pregnant, we had a Morrison-type shelter delivered which we could use indoors. No matter where you went during a raid you never really felt safe. My school pal Ronnie Clarke (the trench-digger) and his family were killed in an air-raid. They lived on the corner of Hill Road and Rotterdam Road and they were all in their Anderson shelter during the raid when a bomb hit the shelter. If they had been indoors they'd have been safe – but that was what wartime was like.

In time we became used to the raids. I could tell from the sound of the aircraft engines if they were 'ours' or 'theirs'. When the daylight raids started if you were outside and you heard the 'plane you could look up as you ran for shelter and actually see the bomb doors open and the bombs come out!

After the raids I (and plenty of other youngsters) would be out collecting bits of shrapnel, the tails from incendiary bombs and cannon shells. Much sought after souvenirs were the three-cornered pieces of metal which some of the bombs contained. These would be scattered all over the place. They were designed so that they always landed with one point upwards to puncture the tyres of fire-engines, ambulances and other vehicles. Like everything else, souvenir hunting was not without its hazards. I remember once, in Old Nelson Street, my brother saw the tail of a bomb sticking out of the ground in the front garden of Mr Morling's house. He climbed down into the crater and started pulling on this tail, trying to get it out for a souvenir. I didn't go down, but stayed up top and watched. What we didn't realise was that it was still fixed to a bomb! Fortunately he couldn't move it and we went home.

Just as we were going down the steps into our house at the top end of the street, we saw the young maid trying to get into Morling's house to do the cleaning, but she couldn't get in, so she left and walked up Old Nelson Street. Just as she got abreast of the Congregational Church – whoomph! the whole lot went up – so did Morling's house! She and my brother were the luckiest people alive.

Old Nelson Street suffered a lot of damage during the air raids and although my house was never hit, we were eventually forced to move out because of blast damage. We had to go because the whole gable end was opened up as if somebody had just put their hands into a crack and pulled it apart! All the windows were blown out and the ceilings damaged. The family and I were down the shelter at the time and when we came out the house was in ruins. Mother just stood there crying, heart-broken. I was completely shocked. Afterwards I think my father went into the *Spread Eagle* with the landlord and got stoned!

We put the furniture into store in a big warehouse at the back of the Market Inn and took temporary accommodation at 39 Arnold Street. The rent was a bit high for us so we moved out of our back gate, into the back gate opposite, into 36 Tennyson Road. The house was right opposite the mortuary and I often used to see the dead being carried in and out. This was at the end of 1941.

The worst raid Lowestoft had was known to the locals as the Waller's raid and was

Oulton Road, where my cousin Stella lived, was surrounded by fields during the war. We used her shelter at night for a while but I doubt if we were any safer there.

The devastation caused by the 'Waller's Raid', looking south along London Road North from Hepworths. The spire, centre top, is where the Baptist Church stood. Boots now stands on the site.

on 13th January, 1942. I remember it well because I had just cycled past where the bomb was to fall. It was snowing and a German fighter bomber shut off his engines, came gliding in and dropped his bombs on the main shopping area. There was no siren sounded so no-one took shelter. Records show that Boots, Wallers Restaurant, Morlings, Bonsalls, Freeman Hardy and Willis, the Fifty-shilling Tailors and Davis the dentists were all destroyed. During this raid fifty-one civilians were killed, eighteen service men and one person was never found.

When the Americans started their one-thousand plane raids, my mates and I would stand and watch in wonderment as they formed-up over the town ready to fly across to Germany. These 'Flying Fortresses' would fill the whole sky with white smoke trails as they manoeuvred; then fighter planes would come in packs to escort them and away they would go. The whole town literally vibrated with the low roar of their engines — day in and day out this would happen.

We would see them return in dribs and drabs, sometimes one flying low and slow over the town — perhaps with two or three of its four engines stopped, or with the nose or tail shot away — I'm sure many watchers on the ground offered up a silent prayer for the crews who were trying desperately to return to the safety of their base.

As the war dragged on so my old boyhood haunts changed. Not long after the outbreak of the war the army fenced them all off — suddenly I couldn't get on the North Extension or the Denes, even the old pickling plots were out of bounds. I can remember my mates and I standing as close as we could to watch as mines were laid, pill-boxes built and barbed wire strung everywhere. There was a 'secret' path through all these hazards. It was through Boardley's yard at the end of Nelson Road and across to the North Extension. This was only for the use of authorised people with business on the market.

Because there was no fishing, my father was employed building air-raid shelters (he helped with the big shelter down on Battery Green — our front railings went into the building of that) and sometimes he would be down on the harbour beach. That's how I got to know of this path because I used it to take his grub to him. I couldn't get on the harbour as I'd always done because a pass was needed. From time to time my father did manage to get out and do a spot of long-shoring — not fishing, but shrimping, between the piers — and they painted big letters on the side of his boat for identification.

Two of my wartime friends were 'Tich' Wilson and John Wooley. They were nearly always with me when I wasn't at work and many were the adventures we had together. Sometimes we would cycle over to Beccles to go swimming and girl chasing. Beccles swimming pool was part of the river that had been fenced in, but at the bottom of the fence was a hole just large enough to swim through. I remember that once we dived into the pool and Tich did not surface. John and I dived back and saw Tich's legs sticking out of the hole in the fence into which he was tightly wedged. John grabbed his legs and pushed him through the hole to the safety of the river. I followed him through and as I surfaced I heard shouting and before I realised what had happened I received a terrific whack on my head which sent me reeling. Unbeknown to me I had surfaced close to a rowing boat occupied by a sailor and his girlfriend — the whack on my head had come from one of his oars as he tried to avoid me. After making sure I was all right he went on his way. Although I told him I was okay to be truthful I did not feel too

The Odeon, 1950. Evacuees from Essex were billeted here *en route* for the Midlands when it was found that Lowestoft would be too dangerous. This building had to be used as a mortuary for a few days in January 1942 after Waller's raid when seventy people were killed.

Sea defences on the North Beach. This was where I wandered with two friends through a minefield, having heard a rumour about butter being washed-up on the beach.

good, so we all went back to the pool, got dressed and then went to our bikes for the ride home.

This obviously wasn't our day, for on the way home we were stopped by some soldiers at a road-block for our identification cards. Unfortunately I could not stop as my bikes never did have any brakes, so I just had to keep going, at the same time calling out, "Keep out of the way — I 'int got no brakes!" I sailed by the startled soldiers and finally came to a halt some way further on by using my tried and tested method of stopping: the sole of my boot on the back tyre! Sheepishly I then returned to the road-block so the soldiers could check my identification.

As boys, we didn't always appreciate the dangers and once, having heard that a cargo boat had been sunk off Lowestoft and that a load of butter had been washed up on the beach, Tich, John and I decided to go down onto the North Beach to look for it, or anything else that might have been washed-up. We walked along the edge of the Denes towards Sparrow's Nest. About halfway along we found a gap in the barbed wire and through it we got onto the Denes and made our way towards the sea wall. About half way across we heard someone shouting and looking back we saw some chap in a peaked cap, together with three or four sailors, waving their arms about. We ignored them and carried on to the beach. Much to our disappointment there was nothing at all to be found. On the way back we met our friend with the peaked cap and his companions. They collared us and gave us a real shouting at — the air was blue. Apparently, on our journey we had wandered through a minefield!

It was while I was working for Stan Button that the biggest tragedy in my life happened. On September 12th, 1942, my mother, whom I idolised, died in child-birth. She was forty-one years old. I was devastated and life became very bitter for me.

After my mother's death my aunt looked after my young sister Meryl, who was only five years old, and I was left with my father and my younger brother Charlie as George joined the Navy and went away.

During the war years I was a member of the Navy League Sea Cadet Corps. Some of my happiest times were spent with the cadets. I started off at Gorleston Road School but later moved to the Denes Oval where we came under the Royal Naval Patrol Service in *HMS Europa* at Sparrow's Nest. We also had a social club near Southwell Road at the other end of town. As I remember, our officers were Captain Tyrell (who was the Lowestoft Harbour Master) and Ken Hutson (a local butcher). The most popular officer with the cadets was Lieutenant Holbrook. We also had instructors from the *Europa*, and through them we had all the training and facilities that were available to the men of the Royal Naval Patrol service who were stationed in the town.

I particularly remember the happy times spent at Covehithe Gunnery School trying out the guns on the cliff top. On one occasion we fired at a drogue target being towed by a 'plane. When we examined it after it had been released and fallen to the ground there wasn't a hole in it, despite the fact that everyone had fired at it!

It wasn't all fun in the cadets though. Many of my school mates and friends died during the war — killed by bombs or enemy action. When I heard of my pals and their families being killed it used to make me feel angry and frustrated and at times I desperately wanted to join the Forces so that I could hit back. It all sounds a bit crazy now but that's the way it was in those days.

Naval cadets and WRNS at the Covehithe Gunnery School. Jack Rose on the right.

War-time Lowestoft with barrage balloon defence against low flying aircraft. A Bofors anti-aircraft gun was sited in the grounds of the Royal Norfolk and Suffolk Yacht Club and the gunners accommodated in the Nissen huts.

During the war Gunton Hall was used by the army as a special training unit for ex-prisoners, borstal boys and lads who couldn't settle down to army life. Tich, John and I became friendly with some of these lads. Their names I have now long since forgotten except for one whom we called Kosbee (from the nickname of his regiment, the 'Kosbies' – The King's Own Scottish Borderers). He became a great friend to us and we were sorry when he was eventually posted away. By an incredible coincidence I met him again a year later when I myself was in khaki – we met on a troop-ship bound for the Far East! When he saw me, his first words were, "Wot, they got you?" They certainly had but the trouble, as far as I was concerned, was that 'they' had put me into the wrong colour uniform! After training with the Sea Cadets for three years I assumed that when call-up came I would be wearing the blue of the Royal Navy but instead I was drafted into the army!

The rear of Old Nelson Street as seen from Whapload Road. In the foreground is the Mayor, Major Selwyn Humphrey, standing by an air-raid shelter that has been blown out of the ground by bomb-blast.

Woolworths was hit by an oil-bomb and destroyed. After the war it was rebuilt in the architectural style of the thirties. On the opposite side of the road the United Methodist Church and Catlings escaped unscathed. The buildings were later demolished anyway and Courts and Gateway now stand on the site.

Army Life

I got my call-up papers in 1944 and asked to go into the Suffolk Regiment and it wasn't long before I found myself on the train heading for Gibraltar Barracks in Bury St. Edmunds. I remember that day well for it was two days before Christmas, snowing and I was frozen stiff! Not having a coat of my own I was wearing my father's overcoat which hung down to my ankles, and my hair was plastered down with old tin brilliantine which resembled green axle grease.

When I got to Bury station we were rounded up by men in uniform, put onto lorries and driven to the barracks. I was taken into a large room with the other conscripts who had arrived with me. There seemed to be desks everywhere, behind each a soldier armed with a rubber stamp and piles of papers. When my turn came to give my personal details I knew exactly what to expect. All my life I had been 'baby-faced' and when I was called-up I looked more like a fifteen year old than eighteen. I gave the clerk my name, age and date of birth. He gave me an old-fashioned look and said, "Are you sure of your age?" I assured him that I was, but he obviously didn't believe me, because instead of receiving my rubber-stamped papers, I was sent out to a barrack room with several other lads.

We had all been issued with our uniforms so we changed out of our civvies, which were packed into suitcases and labelled to be sent home (that was the last we saw of them) and put on our rough khaki serge. We were now just a bunch of 'rookies'. It was bitterly cold in our barrack-room and on my very first day in the army, after dark, some other conscripts and I went to a railway coal depot at the bottom of the barracks where we helped ourselves to great lumps of coal which we sneaked back to our hut in order to try and get it a bit warmer.

The following morning I went to a corporal and asked him why I hadn't been given a number. He told me, as I suspected, that the army doubted that I had given my true age and that they were checking up on me. In the meantime, instead of writing my army number after my name and rank, I had to write N.Y.A. for 'not yet allotted'. A few days later, when they discovered I had told the truth about my age, I was given a number.

Then followed six weeks of basic training and the seemingly never-ending fatigues. When this training was finished we were given a weekend pass. During this time I had gussets put into my trousers to give them wider bottoms and half-pleats put into my tunic. When I returned to camp the Regimental Sergeant Major happened to be outside the guardroom and when he saw me he nearly had a baby.

"Get that uniform back to normal and get a hair cut!" he roared, "and I want you back here in ten minutes!"

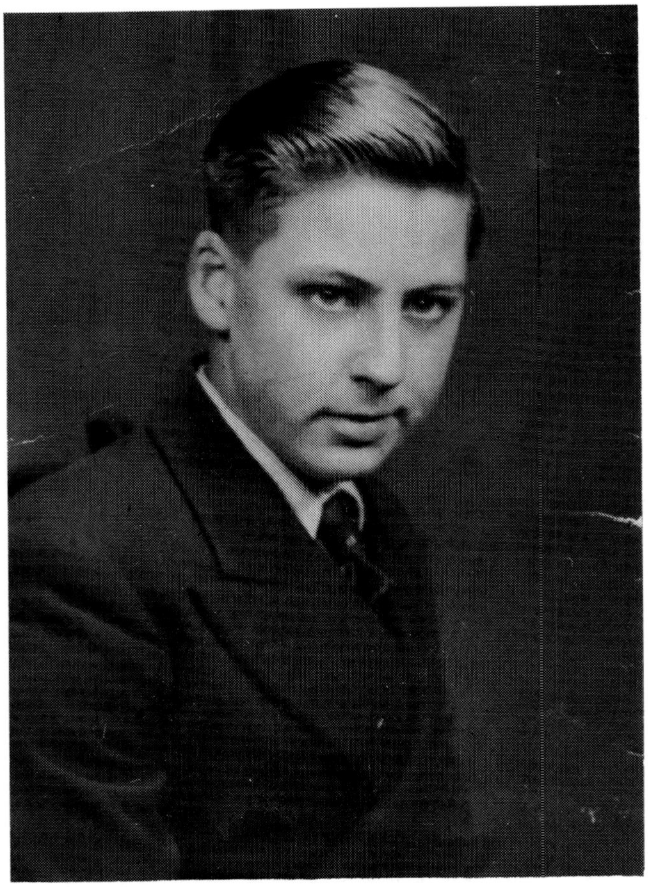

Eighteen years old, just prior to being called up.

One of my postings with the 16th Infantry Brigade, SEAC, was to Chakarata, Mussori, in India.

I rushed over to the tailor and he put the uniform right. Then I dashed to the barber where I finished up nearly bald. I then reported back to the R.S.M. He must have been in a good mood that day because although he bawled his head off at me, calling me a clown, an idiot etc, and threatened to put me on a charge, he took no further action.

After my return I was posted just across the road from Gibraltar Barracks to West Lines Camp, where we had to do another ten weeks Corps training. It was here I met 'Dodger' Allen, one of the strictest Company Sergeant Majors in the army. For all this I was paid the princely sum of ten shillings a week, and from this I sent home two shillings and sixpence to my father. Another sixpence was deducted to cover 'barrack room damages'. This left me seven shillings, but out of that I had to buy all my Brasso, blanco and other cleaning gear that the army thought necessary.

After all the training and tests were finished, I was sent home on fourteen days' leave taking with me everything the army had issued me — including my rifle. When I got home I put my rifle and all my gear into the bedroom cupboard and went out. Returning home later, I went to the cupboard to get some cigarettes, only to discover that my rifle was missing! Panic set in. I dashed downstairs and asked my father if he had moved it, which he hadn't. I realised that only one other person would have touched it, my younger brother Charlie. I dashed outside and down the road and there he was showing it to all the children from round about.

My leave passed all too quickly and I received orders to report to a Combined Operations Centre at Westcliffe-on-Sea. Where we would go from there was secret, all very hush-hush, but when we marched down to the stores and emerged carrying tropical clothing, mainly jungle green, it didn't take much to put two and two together.

I stayed at Westcliffe for a month or two, during which time the lads and I were billeted in empty private houses. We had a really cold winter and, like the troops who had used the houses before us, we made use of the fireplaces in every room. By the time we left there was hardly any wood left. The fences and garden gate had gone and half the floor-boards had disappeared. We burnt the latter by lifting the whole length of board from the floor and placing one end into the fireplace. As it burned away so we pushed it further in until it had all been consumed by the fire!

Finally we got notice to move. On the morning of our departure all the residents of the houses near our billet turned out to see us go and bid us farewell. Being the smallest, and looking like a school-boy, I got the most farewells and hand-shakes.

From Westcliffe we travelled to Liverpool docks by troop-train. At the docks my battalion (with many others) were put aboard the troopship *Brittanic* bound for a destination 'somewhere in the Far East' — it turned out to be India, where we became part of the South East Asia Command under Lord Louis Mountbatten. My regiment formed part of the 16th Infantry Brigade.

During the voyage our time was spent training and having lessons. When our destination was finally disclosed we were given short lessons in Urdu, the main Indian language. We stopped off at Algiers where we picked up two or three hundred French Foreign Legionnaires who were dropped off when we called into Colombo.

Arriving at Bombay we were given a day's shore-leave and after returning to our ship we were transported by lorry to a camp at Deolali close to the birth-place of Mahatma Gandhi where we spent a couple of weeks training and getting acclimatised to our new environment. My platoon sergeant, who had been with us all the way from Westcliffe, was Sergeant Skinner, a Jamaican, and the best sergeant I met in all my army career. From Deolali we were posted to various parts of India. I went down to a Jungle Training School at Ranchi, leaving behind not only Sgt Skinner but another Lowestoft pal of mine, Matthew Boardley. There were two other Lowestoft lads in my Regiment in India, although they were both in different companies to me. One was Jack Burwood of Essex Road (his father was Lou Burwood and worked in the Seamen's Mission in Suffolk Road.) The other was a chap named Beales who lived in Kirkley Run.

At Ranchi I was attached to the Sherwood Foresters and what I went through there was nobody's business. There were kit inspections every morning, rigorous jungle training, forced marches, starvation marches, the lot! Sometimes we were marched miles into the jungle and left there, without food or water, to find our own way back. This was jungle training at its worst! We had to learn the art of survival; what plants, leaves and roots you could or could not eat, how to obtain water by cutting through bamboo at a certain place. We had to carry malaria tablets and a tin of water-purifying tablets so that we could drink water found anywhere. We were also told that if we became desperate for water, a piece of cloth could be laid across the top of a container and then a little soil laid on the cloth. If we then urinated onto the soil it would extract the acids and make it drinkable. Fortunately I never got to try this out although sometimes we did use our own urine to shave in. I was really glad when the orders came for me to move on to Dhera Dun and the Bedfordshire and Hertfordshire Regiment.

When our brigade (consisting of three battalions) moved camp we often had to march. On one occasion we marched for over a week, sometimes as much as thirty miles a day. It seemed to me that we had marched right across India! After a gruelling march on the last day we had to clean ourselves up – polished boots, cleaned brasses – the lot and march in at the slope arms ready to settle down at our new camp.

At Dhera there was a big camp for Italian prisoners of war. One night the prisoners broke out and escaped and British troops were sent out to round them up. Unfortunately, many of the men who were sent after them were tough lads who had just returned from the campaign in Burma and instead of re-capturing the escapees they shot them. A special cemetery was built for these men. It was quite large and when I looked around it I looked in awe and amazement at the beautiful carvings on the graves and gravestones and the inside of the beautiful chapel. All of these had been made by the surviving Italians out of odds and ends and scrap materials – all done in memory of their comrades.

Summer was approaching and it would be too hot for us British soldiers, so we were transported by lorry up the Himalayan foothills, through many winding and twisting roads to a place called Chakarata, a hill station near Mussori. Here, way up above the cloud-line, it was much cooler. We lived in huts with corrugated iron roofs and now and again there was a tremendous hail storm – the hail-stones fell as big as golf balls and the noise as they smashed down onto the roof is hard to imagine!

After a while we were moved on again and travelled all over India by train, stopping every so often at different places. Then, in 1946, there was trouble in Delhi between the Hindus and Moslems and we were sent there.

As a result of my initial training with the Bedfordshire and Hertfordshire Regiment I was given a bren gun, a weapon I had become quite attached to and knew inside out and back to front, and carried with me all my army career. So as bren-gunner, together with sixteen more riflemen, I was selected to be bodyguard for our Brigadier.

Often, the Brigadier and an interpreter would have to go out and talk to the rioting Indians and our job was to protect him. We would surround him in a circle, laying down and facing outwards. As bren gunner, I had to lay immediately in front of the Brigadier facing the crowd. Then he would try to reason with the rioters and get them to disperse. If the crowd or mob advanced towards us we were ordered to fire over their heads with a single shot. If this didn't stop them, then I had to fire a burst from the bren over their heads. This usually did the trick but if they still continued to advance then I had to fire a single shot at the legs of one person to bring him down – as a final resort this was guaranteed to disperse the crowd. We had strict instructions that we were not to shoot to kill unless our lives were in immediate danger.

After three years in India I was given a month's UK leave. I nearly cried with joy when I was told and soon I was homeward bound on the troopship *Empire Ken.* We sailed from Bombay, leaving the heat and the monsoons behind and eventually arrived at Southampton. I was sent to a transit-camp at Shirley and from there I caught a train to take me back to dear old Lowestoft. One whole month's leave lay ahead of me and I was really going to enjoy every minute of it!

It was really good to be back in my home town but the month went by all too quickly and it seemed that in no time at all I was back on the train heading for Shirley. When I arrived I was informed that a telegram had been sent to Lowestoft extending my leave by another fourteen days – but it hadn't arrived by the time I left. I was asked if I wanted to return to Lowestoft or stay in Shirley. Naturally I opted to go back home and away I went again!

On returning home my father told me that the telegram had arrived just after my train had left. He had gone down to the police station to see if it was possible to get a message to me. He was told that it might be possible but it would cost fifteen shillings to relay a message through to the stations at which my train would stop. Unfortunately I was just one jump ahead of the message at every station and it never did catch up with me.

My leave did eventually end and when I got back to India I re-joined my regiment which was now stationed at Hydrabad. Before long I was on the move again. The regiment was posted to Delhi where we were to do guard duty at the Viceroy's Palace. However, I never did do any guard duties because shortly after arriving there we received orders to pack our gear again and were taken by lorry to the troopship *Mooltan.* We were being posted to Tripoli.

When we docked at Algiers I found that I was one of the lucky ones whose demobilisation orders had come through so when the regiment disembarked several of the lads and I stayed on board the *Mooltan* which took us back to England. I finished up in barracks at Colchester where I stayed for a few days. My last move in the army was when I went down to Aldershot for 'demob'. There I handed in all my gear and was kitted out with civvie clothes. I had served with four different regiments, the General Service Corps, Suffolk Regiment, Sherwood Foresters and the Beds and Herts Regiment. With my railway warrant safely in my pocket I returned home to an entirely different life.

Even though my posting to Jungle Training School at Ranchi included survival training I managed to obtain the *Lowestoft Journal.*

After The War

After my demob leave was up, I had to find a job — not an easy task in the lean years following the Second World War. Mind you, as an ex-serviceman I was entitled to go back to the job I had had when I was called-up. I did not want to go back into the building trade, on top of which to take my old job back would mean doing something that I would never willingly do — take another man's job away from him. I was young and single at the time and couldn't care less, I knew something would come along.

Lowestoft Labour Exchange could offer me no jobs that I fancied doing or that suited me, so I borrowed Father's old bike and cycled over to Beccles to see what was being offered there. I took a job with the 'Beccles War Agriculture' (although I don't really know why). The work paid £3 a week and consisted of working on local farms and fields with a gang of lads hoeing sugar beet, clearing fields, removing old wartime tank-traps and pill-boxes and other work connected with the land.

One morning after a couple of months of this, I happened to be working up on Corton Cliffs and I kept looking up and watching the drifters and the other ships steaming past. The sea being in my blood, I knew that I wouldn't rest until I got a berth on one of them so I went down to the Consolidated Fisheries office in Lowestoft and signed on as a trimmer. This was against my father's wishes but I went anyway and the next week I was sailing past Corton Cliffs on my first trip, not on a drifter but a trawler or 'Crownie' as the crown boats belonging to Consolidated were known. I'd told the lads working on the cliffs what time I was sailing and there they all were lined up on the cliff-top.

My first boat was the old *King Richard.* Bill Rudrum, otherwise known as 'Hartlepool Bill', was the skipper. He was a good man as were many of them. I took every chance I could to get away around the coasts of England, Scotland and Ireland. I fished out of Milford Haven, Padstow, Newlyn, Penzance, Fleetwood, Douglas on the Isle of Man and I often went across to Ireland to Waterford, Rosslaire, Wicklow and Dunmore right down in Southern Ireland.

I loved every minute of it, visiting all the different ports. At this time my interest in old Lowestoft was developing as I became aware of changes that had taken place in my home town and as soon as I got ashore I would head straight for the second-hand shops after old postcards of Lowestoft. It may seem strange buying Lowestoft postcards in these far ports but when the fishermen used to call in at Lowestoft they would send a postcard home to let the folks know where they were and over the years many of these cards found their way into second-hand shops.

Life at sea was rough and tough and when I was trawling I had more than one close brush with death. The nearest was when I was third hand on the trawler *Grosbeak*, fishing down by the Bull Rock off Southern Ireland. We were hit by the fiercest gale I have ever known. To make matters worse we were close to rocky reefs and skipper Lenny Brown and Mate 'Pud' Everett had to use every bit of their skills to stop us foundering. As darkness came on so the weather worsened. The decks were knee deep in water, the mizzen sail and small boat were washed away, wheelhouse windows were all smashed and the seas were peeling up like sky-scrapers! At times the ship seemed to stop and shudder as the terrific seas smashed into her. In the middle of this I nearly died with fright when, above the howling wind and roaring seas, I heard a tremendous clattering and banging behind me. Despite the conditions I practically ran to the wheelhouse, convinced that the ship was breaking up. There I stayed until daybreak when the weather slowly abated. When I looked out of the window, there laying on the deck and wedged between the case and the side of the ship was a whole sheet of corrugated iron. It must have been blown aboard from the land which was a good half mile away!

Despite the hardships we still had plenty of laughs. Often we would trawl up human bones. I remember once when we trawled up a perfect human skull. Another lad and I decided to play a trick on our chief engineer with it. When he wasn't around we went down the engine room and stuck it over one of the gas-light brackets there then we hid up and waited until he came down for his watch. He'd been oiling around for a few minutes when he suddenly spotted the skull glowing in the dark. I remember his face even now, I thought he was going to have a heart attack. My mate and I got a right rollicking off the skipper over that.

After a while I decided to give up trawling and have a go at drifting and found a berth on the small drifter *Present Help*. Much to my surprise I found that her skipper was my cousin, Dick Turrell, who I lived with as a boy at 17 Clapham Road.

Drifting or drift-net fishing is as hard work as trawling but not so monotonous. If you had a good haul you could run to port with the catch and sometimes, if you were doing the home fishing, this could mean an extra night in with your family. When you were away from home the time was spent cleaning and sorting out your nets. Ripped or torn ones were called 'splits' and these had to go ashore for mending.

When we were in port away from home and weren't sailing, as soon as the work on board was done we went ashore. I'd wander around a bit, go for a drink or visit the Royal National Mission to Deep Sea Fishermen. As often as not some lads and I would be off after the local girls. My first voyage in the drifters was to Lerwick in the Shetland Isles. I'll always remember the Sunday we first docked at Lerwick. What sticks in my mind is the cemetery perched on the hill overlooking the harbour. There was not a lot at Lerwick except for the 'huts'. These were long wooden buildings where the Scots fisher girls lived.

My first trip in the drifters wasn't successful and we sailed back to Lowestoft in debt so I went back to trawling again. I did the North Shields voyage and the home fishing on the *Friendly Star* with skipper Hercules Utting. Later I went on the *Locarno* with 'Hikey' Catchpole and finished up my career as a drifterman on the *Trier*, an old Dutch boat, registered at Lowestoft. Tommy Wadlowe, a Kessingland man, skippered

Shortly after the war at 36 Tennyson Road. All the fishermen had their own style. My Wedgewood blue suit had wide lapels, pleats and a half-belt in the back of the jacket, flared trousers and I was wearing a black shirt, white tie and blue suede shoes.

The steam drifter *Trier* skippered by Tommy Wadlowe, a real gentleman, and the best skipper anyone could want.

her — a born gentleman he was. With Tommy I earned a good bit of money in the home fishing.

I used to love calling in at North Shields for a good time, but it was terrible fishing up there because of the shoals of jelly-fish. The nets used to split the jelly-fish into small pieces, the trouble with that being that their stings were still in the water and when you started to 'scud' (shake) the herrings out of the nets the spray of water sent the stings all over you. After work, when you went below to clean up you were in agony because not only had the stings been on your face and hands but the water had carried them down your oil-skin collar and over your body. Some of the men would go down to the engine room and wash in paraffin and then stand in front of the boiler door so that the heat of the fire would help draw out the itch.

North Shields had a great reputation for its pubs. There was one I remember called *The Wooden Dolly* because it had a life-sized carving of an old fisherwoman. We would go round these pubs for a drink and to pick up a woman, although I hasten to add that this pastime was mostly for the single men. I can honestly say that hardly any of the married men did this. Apart from the odd one or two, in my experience I have found that the married fishermen remained true to their wives and loved their families.

I know that the word 'fisherman' to some people means a drunkard, and I admit that some are heavy drinkers but a lot of fishermen, the strong-willed ones liked I tried to be, will have a drink or two but they know when enough is enough and say, "Cheerio," to the company. It's always cheerio because hardly ever in my life have I heard one fisherman say, "Goodbye," to another — it's considered unlucky.

The last trawling I did was as deckie-second on the old motor-trawler *Pilot Jack* which had once been a 'tosher', the name given to small sailing smacks. My uncle Arco Rose was the skipper but that didn't count for anything. Being a small boat we didn't go out for longer than a week and fished the local grounds, off Southwold or north-about down to Happisburgh or the Cromer Knoll and what they call the Shoals. Sometimes we'd fish off Lowestoft itself near the Barnard Sands. I enjoyed being on the *Pilot Jack*, they were happy times.

It was during my fishing career that I met my first wife, a Scots fisher-girl from Findochty, Banffshire. I married her despite warnings from my family and friends that it wouldn't work. Being young and head-strong I took no notice and ran away from home and married her just the same. The marriage was a disaster right from the start and eventually, there being no children involved, we were divorced.

After the breakup of my first marriage I took solace in drink. I 'hit the bottle' as they say, but fortunately I stayed sober enough in my mind to keep working. It was at this time that I left Lowestoft, although ironically I was always known as 'Lowestoft Jack', and went from port to port following the fishing and wherever I went I had my good times ashore. Often I would sleep rough and finished up in some queer old dives! I remember one morning waking up in a rough old house down by the docks at Fleetwood. As I slowly came to my senses I began to wonder what on earth I was doing and where I was headed. I looked at the company in bed with me, I looked above me and could see the sky through a hole in the roof and I thought, 'What am I doing in a dump like this? Surely I could do better?" and from that moment on I started to change. It was a gradual change. My excessive drinking started to get less and I started

A scene from the herring fishing industry. Here one can see *Fisher Boy* and *Present Help*. I sailed on the latter with my cousin, Skipper Dick Turrell.

Jackora, one of the drifter trawlers I sailed on when fishing round the West Coast.

Lowestoft motor trawler LT1212, *Pilot Jack.* Once a fishing smack, this was the last trawler I sailed in under my uncle Arco Rose.

The Hamilton Dock. My father, Charles Rose (right) and my brother Charlie in my father's longshore boat, *Mica* LT330. All land in the background is now occupied by SLP. Note the beam trawl which was used for shrimping.

to look after myself again, taking a bit more pride in my appearance and eventually I returned home to Lowestoft.

After my return to the old town I met my present wife, Eileen. At the time she was a widow, her first husband, who had been a friend and neighbour of mine during the war years, having been killed in an accident. She was left with two small children to bring up. We palled up together and found that we got along all right so we eventually decided to get married.

Eileen's eldest sister had married my father and was my step-mother so after our marriage my step-mother was also my sister-in-law and my father was also my brother-in-law! For Eileen's two boys my father was not only grandfather but also their uncle, and similarly Eileen's sister was their grandmother and aunt. All a bit complicated!

Eileen when we were courting.

Jack and Eileen on the North Beach with their first child, Jacqueline.

Life After Fishing

Being a fisherman's wife is no fun and Eileen wasn't that happy with me going to sea, but at least it kept the money coming in. Eventually she asked me to find a shore job and so I packed up fishing and went to work on the night shift at Erie Resistors in Great Yarmouth. I stuck this for a month or two, but as my wife was pregnant at that time and I did not like leaving her alone every night I decided to find another job. I would sleep during the morning then look for a daytime job nearer home during the afternoon. By the time our daughter Jacqueline was born I had managed to find seasonal work in Lowestoft with Mortons Foods – I was employed on the pea viners which at that time stood on the waste land, formerly Kirkley Ham, near Horn Hill. After the 'pea-season' had finished I went down to Birds Eye Foods in Rant Score, with my mate 'Scanny' Waters to try for work there. I had been several times before but had never been lucky.

When I went into the office to see John Wainwright, the Personnel manager, I opened his door and called out, "Anyone dead or dying?" Laughing, he asked me why. "Well," I said, "it seems like the only way I'm going to get a job here!"

Fortunately, I had gone there just at the right time because they were taking people on the following Monday and I got a job.

By this time, although I had given up the fishing, I was still involved with the sea through the lifeboat. My family had been members of the lifeboat service in Lowestoft as far back as 1801 with the first 'lifeboat'. The yawls from the beach were used by the old Beach Companies for rescue purposes before the lifeboats and my family served in them as well. All told my family has over five hundred and eighty years combined recorded service with the lifeboat at Lowestoft and many more years served by my great grandfather James Rose and his brothers of which there are no records.

My oldest uncle, George Rose, was the longest serving member of our family with a total of fifty-nine years; my father had forty-six years service, twelve years of which were as second Cox'n. Another uncle, John Rose, had forty-seven years service and the other three brothers all had at least forty years each.

The generation before that saw my grand-father Henry (George) Rose give forty-seven years service (twelve as Cox'n). His brother John completed fifty years as a crewman and four other brothers also had over forty years apiece. Another relation with a proud record of service was a nephew, Harry Burgess, who served for thirty-seven years – twenty-two of them as Cox'n.

From my earliest days the lifeboat played a big part in my family life. As a child I

No. 1 Mummers Cottages at the rear of Tennyson Road where we lived when first married. The tap was on the outside wall and served all three cottages in the row. The cottages had been condemned as unfit for habitation in the 1930s.

can remember that as soon as the 'maroons' were fired we would all dash down to the beach to see the lifeboat launched. In those days the boat was kept moored between two jetties near the North Pier. On one of the jetties was the shed where all the gear was housed; the oil-skins, life-jackets, sou'westers and rubber boots. The lifeboat at that time was the *Agnes Cross.*

I remember my father telling me that when they went down to the south coast to collect her, they had to steam up and down past a nursing home on the sea-front so that the lady who had paid for and donated the boat could see her.

After the end of the war, when my father suggested that I might like to join him in the lifeboat service, I was very pleased and proud, even more so after I had seen the Cox'n, Harry Burgess, and he gave me a place as a crew member. In all I put in seventeen years service, three years of which I served as bowman. I was offered the position of second Cox'n, but declined and soon after resigned from the service owing to a dispute over the drowning on a groyne of an unfortunate young man. That was back in 1969 and is all history now. I was the last of the Rose family to serve in Lowestoft lifeboat service.

I've often been asked what it is that makes a man want to go out in a lifeboat, often in the foulest of weathers, and risk his life to help others. Many lifeboatmen, being modest, will simply say that they don't know. For me, personally, it was the satisfaction of knowing that someone's husband or son was safe to return home and especially rewarding to rescue women and children.

Many of the people who have been in trouble have told me what a welcome sight it is to see the old lifeboat appearing on the horizon, or making its way towards them through the breakers. Unfortunately, for various reasons, you sometimes arrive too late. I have seen people drown only a few yards from the safety of the lifeboat despite every effort being made to save them. Even if you don't know the person concerned, the awful feeling you are left with often lingers for days – it haunts you.

Like everything else, we had some sad, some bad, and some amusing incidents on the lifeboat. On my first boat, the *Michael Stephens,* we were open to all weathers. Right aft was a half-moon shaped cockpit where we all sat on a wooden seat open to the elements – we were never warm or dry. At least we could huddle together to try and keep warm, unlike the poor old Cox'n who stood alone and exposed on a raised platform steering the boat.

It was marvellous when the new lifeboat, the *Frederick Edward Crick,* came to Lowestoft. She had a covered wheelhouse and a cabin for the crew, complete with a little cooking stove. Funny thing was though, I didn't altogether like this added luxury, I still preferred to be on the deck – I didn't like being closed in – somehow I felt safer in the open although I must admit that in extremely bad weather I was only too pleased to make use of the cabin!

I had the honour of crewing this boat home to Lowestoft from Cowes in the Isle of Wight. The crew at that time consisted of the Cox'n, Harry Burgess, Tommy Knott who was the mechanic, Frankie Swan and myself.

When I was a child my grandfather used to take me to the old beach shed, or the 'shod' as the fishermen always called it, near the gasworks. This was used as a sort of

The Lowestoft Lifeboat *Agnes Cross*, in which my father served, going to the rescue of the smack *Lucky Hit*. The two men clinging to the mast were rescued by the lifeboat whilst the third, who jumped overboard, was pulled up on to the North Pier by ropes which had been thrown to him.

The *Frederick Edward Crick*, a 47-foot Watson type lifeboat built at Cowes at a cost of £47,000, arriving at Lowestoft. Jack Rose is at the stern.

club-room for the lifeboatmen. It seemed to be held together with tar, and was adorned with old ships' figure-heads and the name plates off wrecks. Just outside the front door was a small cannon. I can vividly remember the inside of that old shed, it was dark and spooky with a strong smell of salt, tar and sweat!

During the war this historic old 'shod' was used by the military and all the old pictures, name-plates and figure-heads were removed and taken away, never to be seen again! It was eventually destroyed by the army and its disappearance marked the end of an era.

After the war a Nissen hut was erected near the North Sea Wall, just north of the coastguard station. This became 'The Lowestoft Lifeboat and Life Saving Apparatus Social Club', — what a mouthful and surely the longest title ever given to a society or club in Lowestoft!

This building lasted for some years until the club eventually obtained Ayer's old net store in East Street which was partly paid for by one of the members and my old friend, 'Young' Gus Jensen. I became a member of this club when it was in East Street and later, when it moved yet again to premises on the sea wall south of the coastguard station, I took over the post of Honorary Secretary and held it for seven years until I left the club because of the lifeboat dispute. During that time the club flourished and with my private collection of pictures and models the room soon took on a nautical look.

The lifeboat crew have now broken away from the old club and have formed the 'Lowestoft Lifeboatmen's Crewman's Association'. I was made an honorary member of the new association for regardless of the differences we have always remained friends and over the last few years I have helped the Royal National Lifeboat Institution by raising money with the 'Old Lowestoft' slide shows.

Anyway, I have digressed from my story, but with a reason. I was a member of the lifeboat crew when I started at Bird's Eye, and the Personnel Officer agreed that whenever the 'maroons' were fired I could leave my work-place immediately and run for the boat. For that reason I did not have to work on any of the production line machines that needed constant supervision. One day a supervisor put me on a machine on the fish cake line. I told him that I didn't do machine minding, but he would not listen to me. Not long after, one of the lads came in and told me the lifeboat maroons had just gone so off I dashed to man the lifeboat.

When I returned I was told to report to the office. Apparently hundreds of fish-cakes had gone through the machine in my absence without the batter being poured onto them — my job had been to keep the batter filled up and it had run out! I told them that the supervisor had ignored my protests when he had put me on the line and I was sent back to the factory and he was reprimanded.

During this period at Birds Eye I did a spot of everything — I even saw the ghost in the old building in Rant Score. The late Billy Crouchen and I sat at the top end of the building one night having a crafty smoke (I smoked a lot in those days) when in the dim light of the building we saw a white figure coming towards us. Without a word we both jumped up and quickly stubbed our cigarettes out, thinking that it was a supervisor. Instead of coming right up to us whoever, or whatever, it was turned abruptly and disappeared through the wall!

I muttered to Bill, "Did you see that?"

"Yes," he said, "whatever was it?"

"I don't know," I said, "but I think it might have been that old ghost that everyone talks about around here."

At that time a number of people had claimed to have seen a ghost in Rant Score and the subject had become quite topical.

"What's he doing here?" asked Bill.

"Reckon he's come after a kipper," I joked, partly to cover up my nervousness! After some serious debate we decided not to say anything in case we were ridiculed and laughed at but the story is true and the figure, whatever it was, did walk straight through the wall.

Anyway, after the episode with the fish cakes, I was sent down to the fish market to work, and I stayed there for about eighteen years working the 'six-to-two' shift where my job was to move the fish which Birds Eye had bought. Most of the year it was trawl fish but during the home fishing it was mostly herrings. The work was hard, especially in the herring season, when we sometimes had to work until the early hours of the morning but always started at 6.00 am. We called it the 'six 'til when' shift!

As the years passed the fishing gradually dwindled. The once grand herring season faded to nothing and as fishing quotas were introduced so the trawling also slowed down and the quantity of fish sent up to the factory from the market got less and less. One day the 'plaice contract' was signed with Holland and the lorries loaded with imported fish started to roll through the factory gates.

Just after this my time finished at Birds Eye and the following month many more men received their redundancy notices. After being on the dole for a while I managed to obtain a job as a temporary caretaker, working odd days and weeks travelling round the local schools and filling in when the permanent caretaker was ill or indisposed.

A few months later I was given a permanent post as caretaker at Pakefield Middle School. Mr Taylor, the Head Teacher, is a real gentleman and a man I could respect. He and his staff were very good to me, as were the staff at every school in which I worked. Mr Fielding, the Deputy Head, is another good man, and I had a lot of respect for Tim Mitchell, the woodwork teacher who was a good friend.

I enjoyed going out into the playground and either talking or playing with the youngsters and I think we all understood one another. I found I could mix well with the children and they seemed to get on well with me.

Although I was very happy at Pakefield School it was a long cycle ride from my home in Crown Street. It wasn't so bad in the summer, but when the winter came it made the journey seem twice as far and three times as hard, especially cycling up Kirkley Cliff. I could almost guarantee that when I got to the bridge it would open, and so would the skies — either with rain, sleet, hail or snow — it just seemed to wait for me so that when I finally arrived at work I was soaking wet and thoroughly fed-up! Eventually I decided that I had to find another job, nearer home.

Luckily a vacancy for a caretaker arose at Roman Hill Infants School just down the road from me. Like a shot I applied for it and after an interview with Mrs Scollard, the Head Teacher, and my supervisor, I was fortunate enough to get the post.

My move to Roman Hill School was the best move I could have made. Mrs Scollard always treated me fair and square, and during the time I was at the school I think she got to know my funny little ways. My nine years at Roman Hill were extremely happy, and in the language of an ex-fisherman I can honestly say that there I found myself a good berth on a good ship with a first-class skipper, mate and crew although I must admit that at times the cargo could get a bit troublesome!

I loved all the children at that school and tried to treat them as I would my own grand-children. To my mind they are still only babes and what kind of world they will have to face when they grow up is anyone's guess. Personally I hate to think about what lays ahead of them. While they are young they are enjoying a life-style far better than the youngsters of my generation but I think that they are going to have a harder adult life if the world carries on the way it is.

All good things must come to an end and on my sixty-fifth birthday in January 1991, I retired as the caretaker, or as it was called by then, the 'school custodian' (although to me I was always 'the caretaker' and will always look on the position as such) at Roman Hill Primary as it now called. It was a sad day for me.

The day before I left there was a special assembly laid on in my honour, attended by governors, staff, dinner ladies and helpers. All the children were there in the main hall of the school to say goodbye and to present me with cards and gifts.

One of the teachers, Miss Roots, even composed a song about me which the children sang to the tune of *'She'll be Coming Round the Mountain'*. It took a tremendous amount of effort on my part to stop the tears from flowing that afternoon, especially when all the children in the school queued-up for a hug! After the children went off home I was taken upstairs, where a real feast had been laid, and Eileen and I were treated like royalty.

There they all were, the school governors, the Head, the Deputy Head, and all the staff — there were even a couple of my supervisors! There was wine and a beautiful cake made in the shape of a book and iced with the words 'Jack Rose's Lowestoft'. Then came more gifts and cards — I was totally overwhelmed by it all but that wasn't the end.

The next night, Thursday 24th January, my dear wife Eileen, gave me a tremendous retirement party at the Railway Social Club, Commercial Road. All my family were there together with a few teachers and close friends. Ivan Bunn and his lovely wife, Lesley, brought along their band which everyone enjoyed immensely. As my mate Trevor Westgate remarked, it was just like an old-fashioned 'smoker', only without the smoke!

The biggest embarrassment of the evening (perhaps the biggest in my life) was the arrival of the 'Stripper-o-gram' girl laid on by my boys. What a shock! One that I don't think I'll ever quite recover from.

I thought retirement would be great, but I was in for another surprise. I found that I missed the old school, the company of the teachers and particularly I missed the children. I kept thinking every day was Saturday. In all honesty, for the first few weeks of my retirement I was down-right miserable.

Determined not to get into a ruck, I started to concentrate on all those things I had longed to do whilst at work. I compiled and sorted my notes and books and sorted out postcards and slides. In particular I am now researching and preparing slides for a 'Wartime Lowestoft' show, something I have always wanted to do but lacked time for previously.

Slowly I am getting into a new routine but I can't accept the fact that I am now sixty-five years old and an old age pensioner. Other people become pensioners, not me. I suppose I'll come to accept the idea eventually just like everyone else has to but I intend to do something more with my life as yet, because one never knows what's just around the corner or what tomorrow might bring.

Changes

It was while I was on demob leave that I first became really interested in my old town. Strangely, this interest was prompted by the devastation wrought by the air-raids during the war.

As I wandered round Lowestoft, especially my childhood haunts, gazing at the empty spaces created by Hitler's bombs I soon discovered how quickly you forget the things that only a few years earlier had appeared so familiar.

I then started to tour the junk shops buying postcards, pictures or anything else connected with the town. When I was fishing with the herring fleet, every time we put into a harbour I was soon ashore looking for old Lowestoft postcards. These places were a treasure trove of Lowestoft stuff because when the fishermen who lived there were fishing out of Lowestoft they always sent postcards home to their loved ones.

Once I got started with my collecting, there was no stopping me — I became well and truly hooked. After a while just collecting the pictures wasn't enough, I wanted to know more about the old places that they illustrated and so I started on historical research and the beginnings of an interesting and worthwhile hobby.

I carried on in this vein for a fair while, quietly amassing quite a good collection of photographs and postcards, but it wasn't really until 1969 when I resigned from the lifeboat service that I got the chance to indulge myself more fully in my hobby.

It was during the 1950s, at the same time that I was collecting my photographs, that I became involved in what is now the 'Lowestoft and East Suffolk Maritime Museum Society'. With my interest in old Lowestoft and the fishing industry, it was only natural that when my friend Captain Darnell, the Harbour Master, advertised in the *Lowestoft Journal* his intention of forming a society for sea-lovers, I was one of the first to join. This was back in 1953.

Our first meetings were held in his house and then at the Fishermen's Bethel on Battery Green and among the founder members I remember were the late Bill Solomon, Jack Mitchley, David King and Eric Porter. The original name of our little group was the 'East Suffolk Marine Society' with the main aim of collecting and preserving information, pictures, models or anything which had maritime links with Lowestoft. From then onwards the Society grew and prospered.

Eventually we decided that the Society should have a museum and in 1968, thanks to the hard work of Bill Solomon and another great friend of mine, Roy French, they managed to secure the old church warden's cottage in Sparrow's Nest which was converted into a museum to house the ever-growing collection of maritime memorabilia.

St Margaret's Church. When the late Hugh Lees heard that many of the gravestones in St Margaret's churchyard were going to be dug up and removed he said that it would a good idea to record all the inscriptions before they were lost for ever. I decided to do this and eventually I copied nearly five thousand inscriptions in the eight acres of land that make up the churchyard and presented the results to Hugh as a birthday present! Copies are now at the church and in the files of the Suffolk Genealogical Society.

Mariner's Street looking east towards Mariners Score. On the far left can be seen the old *Mariner's Inn* built in 1521.

When the museum was extended in 1978 the new exhibition room was opened by HRH the Duke of Edinburgh and named in memory of the late Bill Solomon.

Bill Solomon deserves a special mention. He had a keen fascination with the town's fishing history, not so much with the buildings but more with the fishermen and the ships that they sailed in. I am proud to share with Bill the Community Award which was presented to us at the Victoria Hotel by the Lowestoft Rotary Club.

It was during this period as I became more and more involved in the history of Lowestoft that I first met a man who became not only a good friend but also a teacher and mentor. This was of course the late Hugh Lees who during his full life made a great contribution towards the recording of the town's history. Above all else Hugh's knowledge of the history of St. Margaret's, our beautiful parish church, was without parallel and his book *The Chronicles of a Suffolk Parish Church – St. Margaret's, Lowestoft* remains the definitive work.

By the late 1950s the cold winds of change were beginning to blow through Lowestoft, and neither I nor anybody else at that time could have guessed what havoc would be wreaked on the town in the name of progress.

For me the 1960s were the saddest years, being a time of great change in Lowestoft – for the worse, unfortunately. I watched all my old boyhood haunts disappearing and could do nothing about it. No one seemed to care or worry, it was just accepted as 'progress', but to me it was sacrilege. There were a few murmurs of protest but nothing on a scale which would make the Council change their minds. During the 1960s the elected representatives of Lowestoft managed to do to Lowestoft what Hitler had failed to do in the 1940s!

Ancient buildings were bulldozed and flattened left, right and centre and old Lowestoft disappeared before my eyes. I think perhaps one of the saddest sights for me was to see the old *Mariners Inn*, in Mariners Street, come down – built back in 1521. For many years it was the home of the Hembling family then in later years it belonged to Mr Woolner the builder. A member of the Hembling family gave me a lot of details about the history and legends of the old house, the tales of secret passages and cellars and a secret room in which local men would hide when the Royal Navy press-gangs roamed the streets looking for 'recruits' – now gone forever.

Then the old 'Beach Village' went. It was not as many people think the oldest part of Lowestoft – this is the High Street area round the Town Hall, from the lighthouse down to Old Nelson Street. Nevertheless, as the 'Beach Village' grew up on the Denes in the early nineteenth century it attracted the mariners and fishermen and by the end of the century it represented everything, both good and bad, associated with the sea and the fishing. It was a 'fishing community' in every sense of the word.

What a tourist attraction the old village would have made, with the fishermen's cottages, smoke-houses, fish-yards, and net stores, not to mention the pubs! It's a pity that the councillors didn't have the foresight to do something like this instead of just tearing it all down.

Seeing so many of the old places being demolished and the whole character of Lowestoft slowly changing only helped to increase my interest in the history of the town and I decided to join the 'Lowestoft Archaeological and Local History Society'.

The chairman at that time was my friend, the late Peter Harris — a founder member of the Society.

One day when I was chatting to Peter I told him of my hobby and my photographs — I'd never really mentioned it to anyone before. Later he came to my house and I showed him my collection. He was astounded at the amount of stuff I had got together and suggested that I get some of them transferred onto slides and give public shows. "People would just love to see these," he said. He couldn't have been more right.

Over the next few months, usually on a Sunday, my friend George Davis would come round to my house with his camera and slowly between us we got the pictures transferred onto slides. George gave up an incredible amount of his spare time to do this but would never accept anything in return. Finally, I had enough material on slides to put on a presentable show.

The first 'Old Lowestoft' slide shows were at the Trinity Methodist Church, opposite the lighthouse. Initially I was very nervous about standing up in front of people and talking, but with the help and encouragement of John Fuller (he operated the projector while I stood out the front and did my bit) it wasn't too bad. I always felt confident and at ease with John there and found that it wasn't really hard to talk about a subject that I loved so much.

The money raised at these early shows went to the Archaeological Society to help their funds and such was their popularity it wasn't long before I was being invited to give slide shows all over the town for different organisations and charities. It was then that my friend Colin Bryant, a brilliant photographer, started to do my slides and in later years the photographs for my books.

A year or two later it was suggested by the Archaeological Society that I gather together all the information I could on old Lowestoft and put it into a little booklet, a sort of historical guide to the town, the proceeds from the sales of this booklet going to help boost the Society's funds. Entitled *Lowestoft Then and Now — A Walk in the Past* the first edition was published in 1973 with the help of Joyce and David King who together with John Allen reeled it off on a duplicating machine. Since then the booklet has been enlarged, revised and reprinted many times with illustrations by Paul Durbidge, and later a selection of old Lowestoft prints.

Thousands of these little booklets have been sold, and in the 1988 re-print it says "The 1988 re-print will include the 10,000th copy of the second edition of this booklet." It gives me great pleasure when I see someone wandering up the High Street with one of these booklets in their hand.

The first edition was an instant success and every single copy was sold in one night at a show I gave with Bill Solomon to raise funds for the Archaeological Society and the Maritime Society. This show was one of the first that I did at the Sparrow's Nest Theatre (another fine historic Lowestoft landmark that only this year has been demolished after years of neglect by those responsible for its up-keep). At that time the theatre seated 1,066 people and I am quite proud of the fact that on that particular night we managed to fill the old place and in later years I filled it five times on my own.

I've given seven or eight shows at the Nest and in 1982, when the seating capacity had been reduced to around 800, I gave a show together with Bill Solomon's son, Brian and such was the turn out that we were reluctantly forced to turn away over one hundred and fifty people.

I have lost track of exactly how many of these slide shows I have given, but they have taken me far and wide, not only in Lowestoft but also in the surrounding villages. Thousands of pounds have been raised for churches, hospitals, schools, guide dogs, the Heart Foundation, Royal Naval Patrol Service and many, many more worthwhile causes. For my efforts in raising money for them I was made an Honorary Member of the Lowestoft Archaeological and Local History Society.

I enjoy doing the shows immensely, not only because they raise money for worthwhile causes, but also because I get to meet people from all walks of life. The older people love to reminisce and it is through them that I often pick up snippets of information concerning the old town, which I check out afterwards in order to confirm what I have been told. This helps to increase my knowledge of Lowestoft.

Some bits and pieces I write down on paper but the biggest part of the information remains in my head, so I suppose when I die most of it will go with me! That is one of the reasons I have written books on old Lowestoft and put photographs in the local press; hopefully to pass on and share at least some of my knowledge with others.

It was through my involvement with the Lowestoft Archaeological Society that I helped to set up one of the first museums in town. It was in the old laundry buildings in The Prairie (yet another victim of the town's progress). The museum there was opened by Alan Lark, the Mayor of Lowestoft back in 1972. When it was finally forced to close because of the redevelopment of the area, the museum was moved to the Broad House in Nicholas Everitt Park, Oulton Broad where it was formally opened by the Queen on 1st August 1985 and my wife and I were invited to attend.

Back in the 1970s, in August 1974 to be exact, I became a founder member of the steering committee of what would later become the 'Suffolk Genealogical Society'. Under the guidance of Katherine Bardwell and Hugh Lees the Society slowly took shape. For the first six months we all met in Hugh Lees's house, then in January 1975 we moved to the old library in Suffolk Road and it was then that the Society became formally established with Hugh as the president, Katherine as secretary and me as the chairman. I am no longer involved in this Society but I am very pleased that it has gone from strength to strength.

In January 1979, I helped start the 'Old Lowestoft and District Society' with the aim of promoting interest in the town's past through pictures and talks.

Despite many ups and downs this Society has lasted for many years and has recently been revived (and named in my honour) thanks to the hard work of John Holmes. Today it still upholds the same aims as before and meets monthly at the United Reformed Church.

My proudest moment was in 1985 when I was asked to help the town prepare the celebrations for 'Charter Day', the centenary of the Royal Charter which gave Lowestoft its Borough status. We gathered all the information we could find about the original presentation of the Charter of Incorporation and then re-enacted it on the anniversary.

With my good friends Trevor Westgate (left) and Wally Holden at the Charter Day Ceremony 1985 when I received the award of 'Distinguished Citizen'.

On Charter Day, August 29th, I was up at the Town Hall for the official proceedings blissfully unaware of what was going to happen, otherwise I might not have gone! As the various speeches were made, Malcolm Berridge, the Clerk announced that he had a pleasant duty to perform. My name was mentioned and I was called forward and Mrs Pat Ramm, Chairman of the Charter Trustees, presented me with a scroll as "A DISTINGUISHED CITIZEN" of Lowestoft in recognition of my 'invaluable contributions' to the town. I wished the floor would open up and swallow me!

I was later informed that had the town still been a Borough I would have been made a 'Freeman'. No matter what they called it I couldn't have been more thrilled and honoured than I was that day.

Another project I managed to get off the ground, not without some chivvying, was the celebration of Armada Day in 1988. This involved the renewing of the old post, known as the 'Armada Post' at the top of Martins Score, which had been renewed every one hundred years on the anniversary of the defeat of the Spanish Armada.

I had hoped to get the support of the District Council in this project, but despite letters sent to them and the local press they appeared totally uninterested, and for a while I thought that nothing would come of it. Then I heard that the Maritime Museum Committee were interested, and they formed a sub-committee under the late Reverend Howard Whyntie and Roy French and accepted the challenge to celebrate Armada Day.

I was co-opted onto this committee and soon we had things sorted out and the renewal of the old Armada Post took place at 11.30am on 19th July, 1988. At a simple ceremony the old post was taken up and removed to the Maritime Museum and the new post was set down. Under it was placed a lead-lined box which contained all the details, together with photographs, etc. An officer from Lowestoft's adopted warship, *HMS Brave*, officially un-veiled and named the post. Also in attendance was Waveney District Council Chairman Peter Hunt.

Gerry Baxter, John Easter and I had decided that dedicating a new post was not enough and so we instituted a local history competition in which all the schools competed for shields, which were presented at the Town Hall after the unveiling ceremony.

That evening at Sparrow's Nest a commemorative beacon, one of the many lit throughout the country, was lit by Councillor Hunt.

★ ★ ★

I cannot finish without mentioning my good friend Wally Holden. I met him back in the early 1970s and we found that we had the same interests.

Wally came to Lowestoft during the last war as a young soldier in the Royal Army Medical Corps. He was billeted in a house in Rotterdam Road and he met a Lowestoft girl, whom he later married. He has made Lowestoft his home ever since.

Although we have not always seen eye to eye, Wally has been a real and true friend to me in more ways than one. He has always been willing to help me no matter what I do. When I give charity shows he is always there in the background giving me support and encouragement. When my work prevented me from getting the information I needed on a particular subject, I could always count on Wally to pop into the library and get it for me.

I owe a lot to Wally, and I sincerely hope that our friendship will last for many more years. Time slips by and we are not getting any younger and so we make the most of our friendship.

Thanks to my interests in the history of Lowestoft I have made many other friends, including David Butcher, Eric Porter, Jack Mitchley, Ivan Bunn, Mary Goffin, Steven Edwards, Gerald Baxter, Bob Malster, John Holmes and John Easter who recorded my videos. Those I have not mentioned I apologise to but thank them all for their help, support and encouragement over the years.

★ ★ ★

This is by no means a full account of my life. I hope what I have written will give the reader a rough idea of the life of a local man, who has been no high flyer, but who has tried to do the best for the town he loves.

My biggest draw-back in life has been my lack of education (I blame myself for this, being inattentive at school) so I am particularly grateful to my good friend, Ivan Bunn, who has spent many hours making sense of my scribbled notes and helping to put them all together in book form.

Finally I would like to thank the people of Lowestoft for supporting my slide shows, for without an audience I could not have raised all the money that I have. Indeed I would not have done what I have were it not for 'popular demand'. I am very gratified by all the people who tell me that they have enjoyed both my slide shows and books. A further selection of photographic memories of the Lowestoft of my lifetime follows on the remaining pages.

I can still remember the fishing smacks from my childhood days, although they were getting fewer by then. In those days they were towed out to sea by a steam-powered vessel and then left to the mercy of the elements — many were lost.

My uncle, 'Ritchie' Rose at the tiller of a fishing smack.

How folk dressed for a Sunday afternoon walk in the 1930s.

1930s children . . .

. . . but the better-off dressed their children like this.

LT1143

◁ Lowestoft Fish Market. When times were hard we would scrounge the herrings that fell from the baskets. We kept enough for our tea and sold any left over by knocking on people's doors.

Cod being sold on Lowestoft Market. Many a time as a child I scrounged a cod's head to make a meal.

◁ The pickling plots, Hamilton Road. Each barrel contained about 600 herrings – which is a lot of fish to be distributed throughout the country.

Commercial Road. The fish lorries waiting for the herrings sometimes queued from beyond Iron Bridge all the way to the Fish Market.

Lowestoft and Scottish drifters in the Hamilton Dock in the 1930s.

A familiar sight in the thirties — the Wall's Ice Cream man.

The North Beach used to be as popular as the South Beach in the 1930s. We spent a lot of time during the holidays here with a bottle of lemonade and a few sandwiches, and not being allowed home until tea time!

Here I'm fishing off the lifeboat jetty, watching a smack, *Crimson Rose*, leave harbour.

Some of the old beachmen that I respected as a lad in the old beach 'shod'.

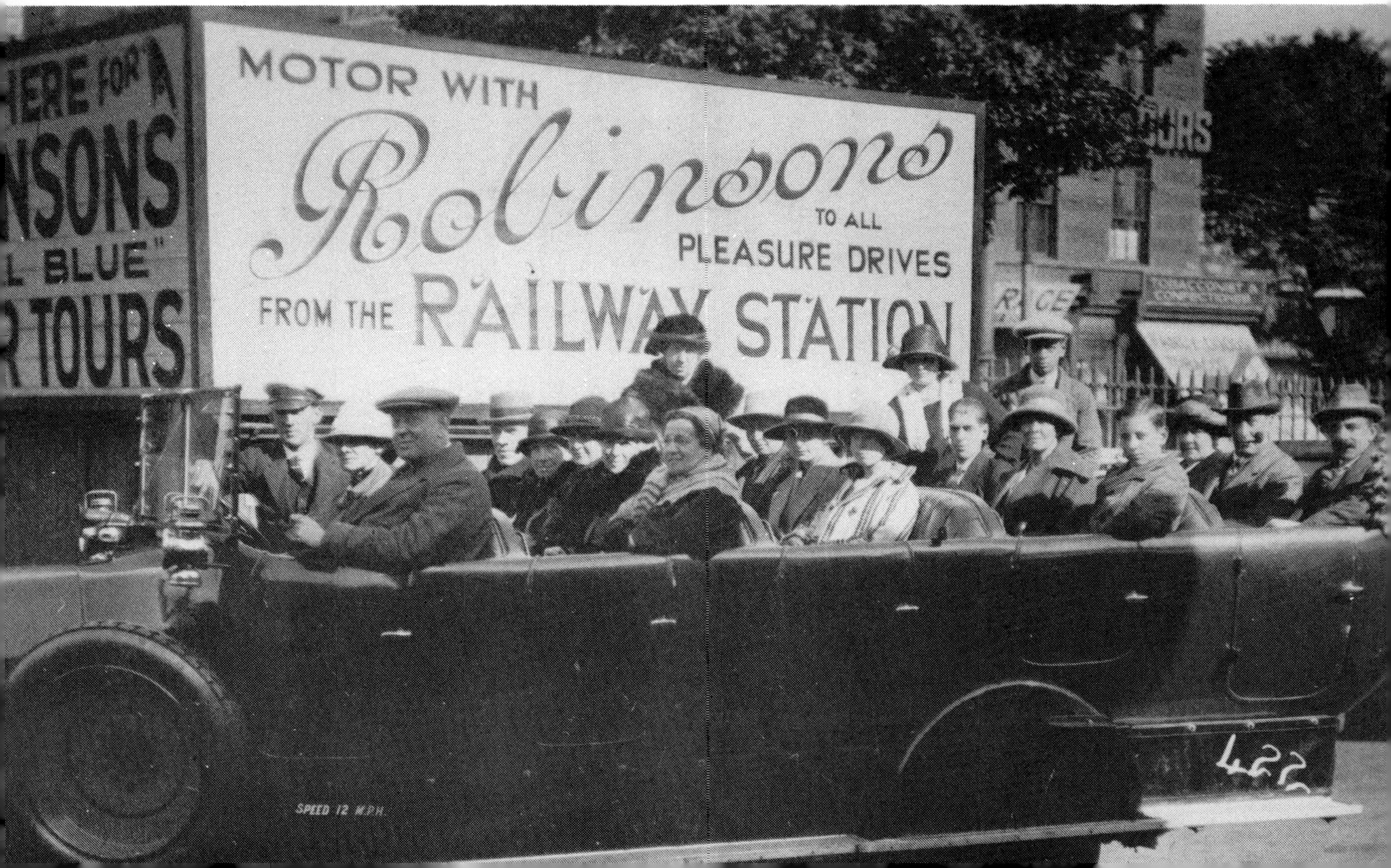

MOTOR WITH
Robinsons
TO ALL
PLEASURE DRIVES
FROM THE RAILWAY STATION
HERE FOR
NSONS
L BLUE"
R TOURS
SPEED 12 M.P.H.

◁ Suffolk Plain in the 1930s, which later became Station Square. The imposing building in the centre top was the *Suffolk Hotel*, long since demolished.

Rogers' Bookshop, which stood opposite to *Lowestoft Journal Office*. It was bombed during the war.

◁ An outing in the 1930s could well have been in a *charabanc*.

Belgian trawlers from Ostend. These trawlers often sought refuge in the port during bad weather.

The United Methodist Church, London Road North. In the 1930s I went to Sunday School here which was held in a small building at the rear of the church, and later served in the Life Boys under Henry Sparham and Harry Chamberlain.

The church was eventually demolished to facilitate the development of London Road North. Courts now stands on the site.

The curious architecture of the Baptist Church in London Road North with its brick and flint *fascia*. The photograph was taken a year before its demolition in 1975 to make way for Boots.

The Lifeboat and Life-Saving Apparatus Social Club, erected near the Coastguard Station on the North Beach and photographed a year or two after the war. When the beach village was demolished the club moved to East Street and then to its present site at Hamilton Road, having changed its name to the Lowestoft Lifeboatmen's Social Club.

IMPORTANT NOTICE

This leaflet is being distributed throughout the country. If invasion comes it applies in this town as elsewhere, but before invasion comes those who are not engaged on useful work should leave this town—see special posters and leaflets.

Issued by the Ministry of Information in co-operation with the War Office and the Ministry of Home Security

Beating the INVADER

A MESSAGE FROM THE PRIME MINISTER

IF invasion comes, everyone—young or old, men and women—will be eager to play their part worthily. By far the greater part of the country will not be immediately involved. Even along our coasts, the greater part will remain unaffected. But where the enemy lands, or tries to land, there will be most violent fighting. Not only will there be the battles when the enemy tries to come ashore, but afterwards there will fall upon his lodgments very heavy British counter-attacks, and all the time the lodgments will be under the heaviest attack by British bombers. The fewer civilians or non-combatants in these areas, the better—apart from essential workers who must remain. So if you are advised by the authorities to leave the place where you live, it is your duty to go elsewhere when you are told to leave. When the attack begins, it will be too late to go ; and, unless you receive definite instructions to move, your duty then will be to stay where you are. You will have to get into the safest place you can find, and stay there until the battle is over. For all of you then the order and the duty will be : " STAND FIRM ".

This also applies to people inland if any considerable number of parachutists or air-borne troops are landed in their neighbourhood. Above all, they must not cumber the roads. Like their fellow-countrymen on the coasts, they must " STAND FIRM ". The Home Guard, supported by strong mobile columns wherever the enemy's numbers require it, will immediately come to grips with the invaders, and there is little doubt will soon destroy them.

Throughout the rest of the country where there is no fighting going on and no close cannon fire or rifle fire can be heard, everyone will govern his conduct by the second great order and duty, namely, " CARRY ON ". It may easily be some weeks before the invader has been totally destroyed, that is to say, killed or captured to the last man who has landed on our shores. Meanwhile, all work must be continued to the utmost, and no time lost.

The following notes have been prepared to tell everyone in rather more detail what to do, and they should be carefully studied. Each man and woman should think out a clear plan of personal action in accordance with the general scheme.

Winston S. Churchill

STAND FIRM

1. What do I do if fighting breaks out in my neighbourhood?

Keep indoors or in your shelter until the battle is over. If you can have a trench ready in your garden or field, so much the better. You may want to use it for protection if your house is damaged. But if you are at work, or if you have special orders, carry on as long as possible and only take cover when danger approaches. If you are on your way to work, finish your journey if you can.

If you see an enemy tank, or a few enemy soldiers, do not assume that the enemy are in control of the area. What you have seen may be a party sent on in advance, or stragglers from the main body who can easily be rounded up.

During the Second World War we received many instructions. I do not know how we would have behaved should the invasion have come.

CARRY ON

2. What do I do in areas which are some way from the fighting?

Stay in your district and carry on. Go to work whether in shop, field, factory or office. Do your shopping, send your children to school until you are told not to. Do not try to go and live somewhere else. Do not use the roads for any unnecessary journey; they must be left free for troop movements even a long way from the district where actual fighting is taking place.

3. Will certain roads and railways be reserved for the use of the Military, even in areas far from the scene of action?

Yes, certain roads will have to be reserved for important troop movements; but such reservations should be only temporary. As far as possible, bus companies and railways will try to maintain essential public services, though it may be necessary to cut these down. Bicyclists and pedestrians may use the roads for journeys to work, unless instructed not to do so.

ADVICE AND ORDERS

4. Whom shall I ask for advice?

The police and A.R.P. wardens.

5. From whom shall I take orders?

In most cases from the police and A.R.P. wardens. But there may be times when you will have to take orders from the military and the Home Guard in uniform.

6. Is there any means by which I can tell that an order is a true order and not faked?

You will generally know your policeman and your A.R.P. wardens by sight, and can trust them. With a bit of common sense you can tell if a soldier is really British or only pretending to be so. If in doubt ask a policeman, or ask a soldier whom you know personally.

INSTRUCTIONS

7. What does it mean when the church bells are rung?

It is a warning to the local garrison that troops have been seen landing from the air in the neighbourhood of the church in question. Church bells will *not* be rung all over the country as a general warning that invasion has taken place. The ringing of church bells in one place will not be taken up in neighbouring churches.

8. Will instructions be given over the wireless?

Yes; so far as possible. But remember that the enemy can overhear any wireless message, so that the wireless cannot be used for instructions which might give him valuable information.

9. In what other ways will instructions be given?

Through the Press; by loudspeaker vans; and perhaps by leaflets and posters. But remember that genuine Government leaflets will be given to you only by the policeman, your A.R.P. warden or your postman; while genuine posters and instructions will be put up only on Ministry of Information notice boards and official sites, such as police stations, post offices, A.R.P. posts, town halls and schools.

FOOD

10. Should I try to lay in extra food?

No. If you have already laid in a stock of food, keep it for a real emergency; but do not add to it. The Government has made arrangements for food supplies.

NEWS

11. Will normal news services continue?

Yes. Careful plans have been made to enable newspapers and wireless broadcasts to carry on, and in case of need there are emergency measures which will bring you the news. But if there should be some temporary breakdown in news supply, it is very important that you should not listen to rumours nor pass them on, but should wait till real news comes through again. Do not use the telephones or send telegrams if you can possibly avoid it.

MOTOR-CARS

12. Should I put my car, lorry or motor-bicycle out of action?

Yes, when you are told to do so by the police, A.R.P. wardens or military; or when it is obvious that there is an immediate risk of its being seized by the enemy—then disable and hide your bicycle and destroy your maps.

13. How should it be put out of action?

Remove distributor head and leads and either empty the tank or remove the carburettor. If you don't know how to do this, find out now from your nearest garage. In the case of diesel engines remove the injection pump and connection. The parts removed must be hidden well away from the vehicle.

THE ENEMY

14. Should I defend myself against the enemy?

The enemy is not likely to turn aside to attack separate houses. If small parties are going about threatening persons and property in an area not under enemy control and come your way, you have the right of every man and woman to do what you can to protect yourself, your family and your home.

GIVE ALL THE HELP YOU CAN TO OUR TROOPS

Do not tell the enemy anything

Do not give him anything

Do not help him in any way

(1649) 59976 Wt. 46381/P1009 250M 5/41 W.P. Ltd. Gp. 8

TOWN HALL.
LOWESTOFT.

17th January, 1939.

DEAR SIR (or MADAM),

The Town Council have been requested by the Government to co-operate in plans which are being made for the protection of civilian life in the event of war.

Recent experience in other countries has shewn that under the conditions of modern warfare, the greatest loss of life is caused by bombardment from the air. This danger is most acute in crowded cities. It is to lessen this danger in case our own country were involved in war that arrangements are being made now to enable children to leave the crowded cities and be received in homes elsewhere. This protection can only be given with the co-operation of those like ourselves who live in the less congested towns or villages. We shall all agree that it is necessary for all of us to help in this plan for saving human life and for safeguarding the rising generation who will eventually have the management of our country in their hands.

I am aware that some arrangements were made last September as a matter of emergency. These had, perforce, to be improvised and sometimes gave rise to criticism; but I am sure that in the light of the experience gained we shall be able to improve on these. The plans for this, as for other branches of defence, must be made in time of peace. We hope that it will never be necessary to put them into operation. But we shall all be happier to know that the plans have been made and if ever they do have to be put into operation the work will be done in an ordered manner and that all will know their parts.

The Government has asked each Local Authority in the country to find out what housing accommodation would be available in case of emergency and what homes would be suitable for those children who would be given the means of leaving the great cities. It is particularly important to know in which houses homes could be provided for the children where they could be lodged, boarded and cared for. Payment would be made by the Government at the rate of 10/6 a week where one child only is taken and 8/6 for each child where more than one is taken. School children would be moved school by school, accompanied by their teachers, and arrangements would be made for the children to attend school in the districts to which they are taken.

A representative of the Local Authority will call upon you some time during the next month or so to find out how far you will be able to assist in this matter. He will produce to you a card, shewing that he is authorised to make these enquiries.

This note is sent to you now in order that you may be aware in advance of this enquiry and why it is being made.

I give you my assurance that the information supplied by you will not be used for any other purpose than that which I have described and that it will not involve you in any work or responsibility unless and until an emergency arises. I feel that I can rely on the people of Lowestoft to offer all the help they possibly can in this important branch of civil defence. It needs no words of mine to convey to you what that help will mean to the children of the big cities.

Yours faithfully,

HAROLD C. BARRACLOUGH,

Mayor of Lowestoft.

◁ Letter about the evacuation of children. Children were sent to Lowestoft from such places as Barking and Dagenham, but Lowestoft, which was severely bombed during the war, was too dangerous for them and they had to be sent on along with Lowestoft children to Derbyshire and Nottinghamshire.

After the war we celebrated with street parties. This one took place in Worthing Road.

▷ I was tossing about at sea during the great North Sea surge of 1953 and it was a fight for survival. The *Guava*, the port's largest trawler, was lost without trace. Ashore, large parts of the town were flooded. Photo shows the corner of Belvedere Road.

Christchurch, once known as the Cunningham Memorial Beachman's Church. To the east of Whapload Road stands what was once the 'Beach Village'.

▷ But when the 1953 floods came, it meant the death of the village which was demolished to make way for an industrial estate. The opportunity to create one of the finest tourist attractions on the East Coast was lost.

The BRIDGE CAFE
Provisions CADMAN Confectionery

August Bank Holiday, 1952. The magnificent Peto terrace, running left to right towards the centre still stands although in variable condition, but the *Royal Hotel* (centre) has been demolished as has St. John's Church. The Victorian pier pavilion, built in 1885, was pulled down in 1955.

London Road North, showing the Methodist Church, now Courts, and Catlings, now Gateway. The building north of Armes was the Y.M.C.A.

Herring Fishery Score, looking from Christchurch. The buildings on the left were demolished to make way for the police station.

A delightful picture. Mrs Bagshaw's shop in Crown Street East.

▷ Chamber's garage in Crown Street West, now Crown Street Motors. As children we watched the men at work making wheels and carts here.

St. Peter's Street in the mid-sixties photographed from St. Peter's Church which was demolished in the early seventies to make way for St. Peter's Court.

▷ St. Peter's Street, looking towards the London Drapery Stores in the High Street (now Harrod's Carpets). The *Triangle* public house on the right was once known as the *Oddfellows Arms.*

CHAMBERS & SON

Mariner's Street, looking towards Mariner's Score. Note the decorative brickwork on the gable of the building in the centre of the photograph.

Maltster's Score. The crinkle-crankle wall on the left has long since been destroyed as have the cottages. Part of the wall on the right remains, although the score is now blocked at the bottom end.

Wilde's Score. As children we used to run up and down all the scores just for fun. Other times we would walk up and down counting the steps.

Once the Borough of Lowestoft ran its own public transport. The 'Corporation buses' were well liked by the local people.

There was also a Lowestoft North Railway Station, hence 'Station Road' near the junction of Corton Road and Yarmouth Road.

Sparrow's Nest — one of our playgrounds. The Royal Naval Patrol headquarters, called *HMS Europa* during the war, is on the left. The Sparrow's Nest Theatre, venue of my slide-shows, was demolished in 1991 after many years of neglect.

Mariner's Score, formerly known as Swan Score from the name of the inn standing at the top where Oliver Cromwell stayed when he 'visited' the town. At the bottom stood the first low light, illuminated by candles. The score went right down to the sea through the 'beach village'. The postcard reproduced here is postmarked August 1933.

The view changed when the 'beach village' was cleared away after the 1953 floods!

Contrary to the belief of many people the Denes have never been common land and records as far back as the reign of Elizabeth I show local people paying a toll to the Lord of the Manor for the right to take a horse, cart, dry nets and graze cattle on the Denes. More recently the area has been used for recreation although some net drying still goes on there.

The photograph, which was probably 'posed' shows men working on a sail which is to be cleaned and tarred ready for use.

At the time of writing controversy rages over the future use of the Denes following an application by Birds Eye Walls to extend their factory. In a few months will a further part of Lowestoft's history have disappeared beneath tons of concrete and steel?